WILD BY NATURE

WILD BY NATURE

True Stories of Adventure and Faith

TOM MORRISEY

Baker Books

A Division of Baker Book House Co
Grand Rapids, Michigan 49516

Published by Baker Books
a division of Baker Book House Company
P.O. Box 6287, Grand Rapids, MI 49516–6287

Printed in the United States of America

Library of Congress Cataloging-in-Publication Data

Morrisey, Tom, 1952–
    Wild by nature : true stories of adventure and faith / Tom
Morrisey.
        p.   cm.
    ISBN 0-8010-1205-8 (cloth)
    1. Morrisey, Tom, 1952– 2. Christian biography. 3. Nature—
Religious aspects—Christianity. I. Title.
BR1725.M54 A3 2001
277.3'0825'092—dc21
[B]   00-068071

Scripture is from the King James Version of the Bible.

For current information about all releases from Baker Book House, visit our web site:

http://www.bakerbooks.com

CONTENTS

Introduction   7

1. Up the Devils Tower   13
2. Into the Devil's Ear   41
3. The Algonquin Bear   59
4. Metamorphosis   81
5. Trying the Triumph   105
6. The Jump Turn   127
7. The Full Spin   147
8. The Keeper of the Winds   169
9. The Legacy   193

Acknowledgments   213

INTRODUCTION

I remember still a cold November morning when my father took me out to shoot a fox that had been menacing the chickens on an elderly relative's farm.

The picture stays with me because I was seven years old that November, and the shooter of the fox was to have been me—the first time, ever, that I would be allowed to fire upon anything other than tin cans or paper targets. I remember how grown-up I felt, waking long before sunrise to put on woolens and hunting clothes, and then eating the breakfast my father had made, the eggs fried crisp in the bacon grease, still sizzling as I carried them to the table. I can still picture us later that morning, creeping on hands and knees over a small knoll and seeing the fox, her coat golden-red against the stark white snow, a vivid contrast even in the gray light of a winter dawn. And I can still feel the .22's wooden stock, smooth and cold as I pressed it against my cheek.

And then I remember the steam rising from the den as two young foxes emerged, more fur than form, wrestling and tugging at one another in a post-breakfast foray. And how my father, seeing this, rose to his feet and shooed the trio back into their den.

Disappointed at having my shot spoiled, I asked why he had done it, and he told me, "We couldn't kill her. She had cubs."

Still dejected, I asked, "But won't they grow up and raid the henhouse, as well?"

And I remember his response.

"Probably," he said. "But they haven't yet, and we need to give them a chance."

From this, I learned that nature and our adventures can teach us things, if only we will open our eyes and our ears—and our hearts—to their lessons.

I remember also the Bible we had in our house at the time, a thick, heavy tome, ideal for pressing leaves and weighting down freshly pasted school projects. When I asked my mother about it, she told me it was God's book, which I interpreted as meaning that it was His personal property, and I was not to be nosing about in it.

Years later, I would understand that I had been correct in my first assumption but 100 percent wrong in the second. The Bible is God's property, but, far from desiring that we stay away, He *wants* us to be nosing about in it.

By the time I discovered this, I would be a man, and I read the Bible secularly several times, treasuring it as the font from which so much of modern literature has sprung. Then my heart was opened to its true nature—that of the greatest love letter ever known, written by the only One Who can love us perfectly. And, like a person with a cherished love letter, I have been reading and rereading it ever since.

This is a book of nine true adventures—things that have happened to me in the course of exploring the twin worlds of nature and sport. That I have had so many is probably due not to my dauntless or courageous nature but to the fact that I am a slow learner—most adventures are, after all, the results of errors in judgment.

In the section following each story, I look at what God has to say on the subject. This is not to say that I am privy to any inside information from the Almighty. But the Bible is a wonderful picture of that part of the mind of God that He desires to be known to man, and the Bible will speak extensively on all manner of subjects if one only has the patience to search it. And, because the Bible is the principle manner in which God communicates with us, any truly God-authored doctrine or fundamental of belief can always be supported by passages from Scripture. That being the case, I mention things said in the Bible often in this book and, when I do, I provide a reference such as this—John 3:16—telling where in Scripture I found the information conveyed.

To those who are new to the Bible, such references may mean nothing (and we have all been there at some point), but they are easily demystified: The proper noun beginning the reference (the "John" in "John 3:16") refers to a section of the Bible called a "Book," and most Bibles will list the page numbers of their Books in a contents page or pages. This is then followed by a chapter reference (the "3" in "John 3:16"), appearing in most Bibles as a larger number at the beginning of a section of text. The final number, the verse number, will be fairly tiny in most Bibles, but will come at the beginning of a sentence, group of sentences, or a phrase.

If you look up the verse we've cited here, you'll find words to this effect: "For God so loved the world, that he gave his only begotten Son, that whosoever believeth in him should not perish, but have everlasting life."

I offer this brief introduction to the Bible because, while the references given may make it seem that it is a companion volume to this book, the reverse is actually true—this book was written as a companion volume to God's Book. The Bible has astounded people with its big ideas for a great many centuries, and if my book opens even one fresh pair of eyes to that great set of wonders, it will have been well worth the writing.

9

One final note. The title of this book comes from Romans 11:24, in which the apostle Paul writes to Gentile Christians living in the city of Rome. In it, he makes an agricultural metaphor, referring to members of the twelve tribes of Israel as the natural branches of the "tree" of God's chosen people and to the Gentiles as branches of a wild tree—a tree that is "wild by nature"—grafted in. Like many Bible verses, this has a modern application if one thinks of those who were raised in Bible-believing Christian households as the natural branches and those who came to belief much later in life (such as myself) as the wild.

Regardless of whether you come from the natural tree or the wild, this book is for you. I offer it with the hope that it will encourage you on the greatest adventure of them all.

For if thou wert cut out of the olive tree
which is wild by nature, and wert graffed
contrary to nature into a good olive tree:
how much more shall these, which be the natural
branches, be graffed into their own olive tree?

ROMANS 11:24

1

UP THE DEVILS TOWER

*Pride goeth before destruction,
and an haughty spirit before a fall.*
PROVERBS 16:18

The giant stone pillar known as Devils Tower, Wyoming, would be remarkable in any setting. In the place where God put it, it is especially so. The low country of eastern Wyoming—that region, say, from Cheyenne to the Montana border—is remarkable for the soft, rolling counterpoint it provides to the Bighorn Mountains and the rugged Rockies to its west. Placed amidst such pastoral surroundings, the weathered-rock citadel is a geological exclamation point, fit to take the breath away.

It was during a road trip through the West that I first saw Devils Tower. Greg Lutz and I had just finished climbing in Colorado's Rocky Mountain National Park, occupying ourselves principally with Long's Peak, the highest mountain in the Front Range and—from the eastern face, at least—one of the most challenging.

Long's had been a victory of sorts for us. The first night on the peak, we had weathered a Rocky Mountain thunderstorm, throughout which the peals had been virtually palpable. For more than an hour, not a second passed during which our little nylon tent did not quake with the sound of thunder. On several occasions, bolts of lightning seemed to have struck within a stone's pitch of our campsite. That we did not retreat was due mostly to the fact that running seemed far more hazardous than staying put. Nonetheless, when the soft and misty morning came, we rose to a sense of accomplishment.

Walking the rocky and still-damp trail that day, we met a Park Service ranger. On seeing our climbing ropes, he had sighed with relief.

"You're climbers," he'd gasped, not so much a question as a hopeful, even desperate, statement.

Actually, the route we'd chosen up Long's for that day was the Keyhole, a hiking trail, but to say that would have been too deflationary. We simply nodded, instead, and he explained that a solo climber was a full day overdue on the Diamond Direct, then the most challenging route up the sheer East Face of Long's. Rangers had gone 'round the west side to see if they could spot him through the cloud-cap at the summit. If they could not, would we be willing to help mount a rescue?

We volunteered for the cause, even though the idea of roping up for an ascent of the Diamond Direct—infinitely more technical and challenging than the route we'd intended—both terrified and thrilled us. We followed the ranger around a giant scree field to Chasm Lake, at the base of the huge, vertical East Face, where he unlocked the rescue cabin and brewed up some cocoa. We shook off the morning chill and listened to the cryptic traffic on the Park Service radio frequency.

Squat and low, the Chasm Lake structure was more properly a hut than a cabin—a pair of cramped bunks flanked by a small table and a stove. As we huddled near the latter, the wind picked up. Hearing it moan around the eaves, I thought of the lost climber, hanging in his climbing harness through the previous night's storm. Lightning had doubtlessly struck the summit countless times, and the cracks climbers follow are natural conduits for electricity. I shook the thought away and sipped my cocoa in the windowless room.

At length, the radio came alive to report that the missing climber had checked in with rangers at the trailhead, having somehow passed in the cloud-cap the party dispatched to rescue him. Our recruiter thanked us for our time, and we hiked back around the scree field with packs considerably lightened by the reprieve.

We were young men, so neither of us talked much about the fear that the prospect of a direct ascent had kindled in us. But our manner showed our joy at being let off so easily; we joked as we made our way up through the steadily clearing mists. Through storms and lost climbers, we had stayed the course, and the residual fortitude helped see us through the scramble to the summit ridge. As we stood there on the roof of Colorado, an ancient DC3 came lumbering slowly up out of Boulder. With a struggle of horsepower heard easily from our perch, it cleared a pass to our north by only a few hundred feet, continuing more gracefully into the easier air beyond. It was a remarkable lesson in elevation, with cloud banks lying well below us and our feet planted on rock so airy that even airplanes had difficulty reaching it.

The ruggedness of Long's Peak and the sheer verticality of its east face had left us unprepared for the soft weathered hills of eastern Wyoming. Even Sundance Mountain, where the Lakota Sioux had attempted to revive their ancient ceremonies before a final, desperate round of battles with federal cavalry, was not so much a mountain as a hill, a flat-topped hummock in an undulating terrain of green. The landscape was dotted here and there by creek-fed trees. Its only inhabitants were long-eared jackrabbits the size of small dogs and—in the soft light of new morning—an occasional fleet and bounding antelope.

That summer, we were driving my first new car, a tiny Chevrolet Chevette painted the same heart-stopping orange that the Air Force uses for marking survival gear. The little four-cylinder engine had labored ceaselessly up to the trailheads in the Rockies and seemed to be enjoying the relative reprise of the Wyoming sage.

We had made only two stops en route. One was just a few miles outside Estes Park, when a scratching from within one of our backpacks alerted us to the presence of stowaways. We'd pulled to the side on a rare turnout in the Big Thompson Canyon and—Greg holding a frying pan in a two-handed grip just in case it turned out to be something venomous—I'd opened the pack's rain flap to reveal a pair of seven-striped ground squirrels, still sleepy from a granola-bar feast. Startled by the presence of two giants (one still wielding the blackened frying pan), our unexpected traveling companions shot from the car and vanished into the roadside scree, strangers suddenly at liberty in an alien land.

Our other stop had been a side trip to inspect the town of Morrisey, Wyoming, a geographic namesake I'd found on the road map and had to see with my own eyes. I was a struggling and nearly penniless graduate student that summer, but even so, Morrisey turned out to be a municipality that I could probably have purchased in its entirety, had I wished to do so. A single worn-out gas station faced a derelict general store, two houses (one unoccupied and one leaning in that direction), and the dilapidated remains of a grain elevator. Hails to the house had produced no response, so we'd returned to the highway and settled back for our ride north.

We had struck camp on Long's at sunrise, quitting the park by late morning. Even so, the West is a land of distance; afternoon shadows were stretching over the road as we rounded a curve in the two-lane. Then we saw it, sharp and dark-shadowed on the horizon.

There are those who describe Devils Tower as resembling a tree stump. And that, indeed, is exactly the impression we had on our first prospect—a tree stump, but a tree stump so dramatically gargantuan that even the mightiest of redwoods, made a hundredfold larger, could never have left it.

Geologists classify Devils Tower as an "igneous plug," a bland and unflattering term that hardly approaches the grandeur of the actual object. It is much more romantic to think of it as the skeleton of an ancient volcano, even though, technically speaking, that is not true. The natural stone citadel of Devils Tower was once the molten core of an upwelling that tried, but failed, to breach the surface and become volcanic. The slowly cooling magma had formed into giant, crystal-like, hexagonal rods, packed tightly together like a giant cluster of pencils. These had stayed buried nearly half a mile underground for millennia, emerging only as the softer surrounding rock weathered and exposed the more robust basalt. It is the cracks between these giant hexagonal columns that give Devils Tower the semblance of bark and its likeness to a giant stump.

The Indian legend as to its formation has, oddly enough, nothing to do with trees. It holds that three maidens prayed for safety when attacked by a giant bear. The small stone on which they cowered then thrust itself mightily from the ground, and the cracks we see today are—

17

according to the legend—the claw marks made by the frustrated grizzly as it attempted to reach its prey.

It was another Indian legend and the white man's interpretation that gave Devils Tower its name. The Sioux believed that thunder originated from the monolith (a belief that is easy to understand when storms rage nearby and peals echo from the rock face). Thunder was, in Sioux mythology, the product of a wrathful god, and early white settlers, on hearing this legend, wrongly ascribed the tower not to its Creator but to the devil.

Seeing the tower in the clear afternoon light put the lie to that. It was too magnificent to be the product of anything but a perfect God. We stopped the car on a pull-off, got out, and just looked for a full minute before Greg lifted his Nikon for a photograph. He pressed the shutter, replaced the lens cap, looked at me, and we both said it at the same time—"We've got to climb it."

Climbing Devils Tower just thirty years earlier would have been the stuff of newspaper headlines. It had been done, after a fashion, in the nineteenth century, when a local rancher had driven fenceposts into a system of cracks and spent months fashioning a wooden ladder to the top (remnants are still there today). That had been a preparation for an Independence Day stunt in which the rancher, circus cape about his neck, had scaled the tower to thrill picnickers below; a pair of twelve-year-old boys then stole the rancher's thunder a few minutes later by following him to the top. But the Tower was not climbed conventionally until the Second World War.

Ascents were once so rare that, in 1947, when a daredevil parachutist named Charles Hopkins landed on the summit of Devils Tower in a publicity stunt, his inability to fashion a rappel for the rest of the journey groundward would spark a rescue effort requiring climbers from two neighboring states and a call for assistance (needless, it would turn out) from the Goodyear blimp. Sustained by air-dropped rations, Hopkins would stay on the summit for two weeks until rescued by climbing legend Jack Durrance, the pioneer who had established the second climbing route up the Tower three years earlier.

Throughout the '40s and much of the '50s, climbing Devils Tower was a bureaucratic labyrinth. The area around it had been declared a National Monument, and ascent attempts required multiple applications submitted months in advance, and written permission from the director of the Park Service himself. But, by the mid-1970s, when Greg and I first visited, ascents occurred so regularly that fixed anchors had been set at two points into the rock face to save the wear and tear caused by climbers driving pitons for their rappels.

Such accessibility (our "application" consisted merely of signing a book in the Devils Tower National Monument Visitors' Center), together with our unearned heroics on— and easy ascent of—Long's Peak, gave us far too light-hearted an outlook about the prospect of scaling Devils Tower.

The two of us would be climbing the Durrance Route, a climb with a rating only slightly above middling difficulty. More stiffly rated routes had fallen easily to us on the West Virginian limestone where we'd trained. It would be, we told one another, a walk in the park.

Dusk was fast upon us as we drove into the National Monument campsite and set up the little two-man mountain tent we'd carried up Long's. Our neighbors were in pop-up trailers and Winnebagos, their generators coughing noisily to life as these more modern "campers" settled down to an evening of television. The last of these had finally died down when a rattle of glass and tin awoke us.

Greg and I looked at one another. The grizzly of Indian legend was not far from either of our minds. Fishing hurriedly in a rucksack, we armed ourselves with an ice-hammer and crept out into the cool Wyoming evening.

19

It turned out to be raccoons—at least a dozen of them, masked and cunning like the thieves they were, tearing open a bag of garbage that had been dropped next to the big, steel, "bear-proof" NPS cans. We shooed our visitors away, put the garbage into the can, secured it, and then watched in amazement as one of the little brigands jumped atop the barrel, gave a lurch against the bail and then, assisted by accomplices, opened it.

Certain that we would get no sleep otherwise, Greg and I retrieved the garbage from the can and carried the bag to the outbuilding containing the rest rooms. There, we deposited it next to the sink while the Lilliputian Merry Men grumbled amongst themselves outside.

We were not, however, to have the last hurrah. No sooner had we left the outbuilding than the king of the thieves was furiously scrabbling at the men's room door. With an effort, he got it an inch or so ajar, and two of his band were there to assist him, pulling at it with all their might. Once the gap had widened to half a foot, a veritable torrent of raccoons poured into the building, their victory announced by the muted crash of tin cans within. Greg and I gaped at one another, then decided to sleep in a bit and let some other camper be the first to shave in the morning.

That midnight escapade, together with our high opinion of our climbing abilities, didn't put us at the base of the Durrance Route until well past noon the next day.

Surprisingly, the scramble up the boulder field had left us a bit winded—something we'd not expected after our days of acclimatization on Long's. Neither of us said anything about it, but we were glad for the rest as we stopped to take off our running shoes and put on the tight-fitting, rubber-sided friction boots used for high-caliber rock-climbing.

And then there was the rock. The stone of Devils Tower is a smooth-faced, dense, igneous basalt, as featureless as the surface of a granite monument. We had done most of our training on West Virginia limestone, which is studded with nodules, pockets, and the occasional ample "bucket" hold. Devils Tower would give none of that—we would be climbing, for the most part, smooth-faced cracks between the Tower's columns, a form of climbing neither of us had done with any frequency. I muted my sigh of relief when we played the age-old children's game for the first lead and Greg's open-handed "paper" wrapped my clenched-fist "stone."

We'd done no research on the Durrance Route, only looked at it from ground level the day before. The initial pitch, or rope length, was up a broken and leaning column. After that, it was straight up to a sloping, grassy ledge—known, with that understated humor special to climbers, as "The Meadows"—across which one could walk to reach any of a number of cracks that led to the top. From the ground it looked, as most climbing routes do, straight-forward and relatively simple.

The first pitch was just that. Greg led out up the sloping column, pausing to put in a chock (the hexagonal artificial chockstones that we, like most modern climbers, used instead of pitons) more out of respect to our elevation above the nearby Platte River than the difficulty of the pitch. As Greg sang out a lazy "B'lay off," I undid my belay-anchor and pulled a nylon-web sling over my head and shoulder for the climb up to join him. My partner called that he was on belay, and I started up, gathering his chocks as I went.

Those who caution others "Don't look down" have never rock-climbed. Climbers do look down, do so often, and I was no exception as I made my way up the leaning column. The lowland nature of the surrounding country meant that we could see for miles—all the way to Sundance Mountain and beyond. I paused and watched the burnished meandering of the Platte, then waved as a sight-

21

seeing Cessna 170 cruised by, just slightly above us, about a quarter-mile out. I was in good spirits, right up to the moment when I topped out on the column and saw Greg's face.

"What's up?" I asked.

"This," he said, looking skyward, and I followed his gaze to a bulging pillar that bellied out slightly and then blocked the view of the rest of the route. That it had been climbed before was obvious—we could see the white marks of gymnast's chalk (an absorbent used by climbers to dry the hands) on the crack to the right side of the column and black scuff marks on the crack to the left. Between the two was a blank expanse of rock that looked to be a good four feet wide.

"Looks as if they stem it," I said. Stemming is a technique used to climb two cracks simultaneously, keeping outward pressure against each one. It's never easy and doubly difficult on an overhanging route.

"I don't envy you the lead," he replied.

That it was my lead went without saying; Greg had led the first pitch and besides, I—the taller of the two of us—would have an easier time leading on the wide stem.

We drank some water, ate a couple of granola bars, and watched small clouds scud in over the top of the Tower as I readied my sling of equipment. Finally, when to wait any longer would be an obvious stall, I stood.

"On belay," Greg told me, more out of habit than necessity.

"Climbing," I replied, wedging a fist into the right-hand crack.

My next move, lifting a foot into the left crack, gave me the feeling that I was about to topple backward. I panted as I tried to better my purchase.

It felt ridiculous—here I was, not two feet from my belayer, worried about plunging from the rock.

"Easy," Greg half-whispered.

I nodded, moved my right foot up as well, and pushed hard with my left hand at the opposing crack.

Falling is part of climbing, but it is not the good part. Earlier that summer, I had taken my first big fall while climbing Conn's East, an easy route on West Virginia's Seneca Rocks. The route was familiar to me; I'd led it several times before. I'd been doing a traverse and had asked my belayer for lots of slack. Near the end, a large hold had beckoned, just inches beyond my reach. I'd leapt for it— and missed.

My feet had caught the ledge from which I'd jumped, flipping me over as I continued down. A dropped body falls, initially, at thirty-two feet per second, picking up speed as it goes, and it seemed that I fell—upside-down, looking out into a topsy-turvy valley and seeing, amazingly enough, a small tombstone beneath an oak tree— for at least a full second-and-a-half before the rope caught me. My climbing hardware swung up and struck me in the face as I dangled a good four feet away from the limestone wall. I'd pendulumed back and forth until I caught a hold and then climbed unsteadily back up to the top of the pitch. Later, from the top, we'd peered at the opposing valley twenty minutes or more before we saw, tucked into the shadows beneath a gnarled oak, the solitary tombstone on which I'd focused during my fall.

I thought of that as I tried to lead the second pitch of the Durrance Route, and the gloom of it all got the better of me. I stepped down onto the ledge next to Greg.

"Okay?" he asked.

"Just need to regroup."

I shook the tingling out of my hands, hopped to restore circulation to my feet, and then stepped back into the cracks, straining and muscling my way up the route. After about twelve feet, I paused and—still certain that at any moment I would tumble backwards—fished out a chock, which I buried deep into the crack in front of me. I held onto its sling and rested before clipping the rope in. It was a breach of form; it would turn our assistance-less "free" ascent into an "aid" route, but I did not care.

Ostensibly, I was now safe—the chockstone would provide a pulley-like point from which the rope could depend, should I fall. But I did not feel safe. I felt exhausted, exposed, and alone.

"Hey, Tom." Greg's voice reminded me of his nearness.

"Hmm?" I looked down.

"We've got weather coming in."

I leaned back on the chock, looked up, and saw clouds— not the small fair-weather clouds we'd seen earlier but seething masses of wind and vapor racing over us, reaching to block out the sun. It was almost a relief.

"What do you think?" Greg asked. "Top out this pitch and work over to a rappel or bail out now?"

As if in answer, a distant peal of thunder reverberated hollowly in the distance.

"We bail," the two of us said at the same time.

Physiologists tell us that the average human being works at only 10 percent of his capacity most of the time. The next few minutes gave us a dramatic demonstration of what happens when the other 90 percent is engaged. As the thunder grew nearer and the wind picked up, I retrieved the chock and half-slid, half-down-climbed my way back to the ledge. There, in wordless coordination, we packed gear into rucksacks, fixed a large stone into a crack as a belay anchor, draped the halved climbing rope over it and—in a matter of seconds—wove in the figure-eight rappel rings we would use for our descent. Even so, the first fat drops of rain were falling as Greg clipped the ring into his harness and stepped over the side.

By the time my turn came, it was raining in earnest. The rock was slippery as ice as I stepped off the ledge and began my rappel. The fierce wind caught the rope below me and whipped it against the rock face as the thunder grew almost continuous. Bright flashes of lightning lit up the surrounding country. Below, through sheets of rain, I saw treetops swaying violently, and I blinked to keep the water out of my eyes.

Half-slipping, leaning into the wind, I made the rappel down to where Greg stood, at the top of the boulder field. We retrieved the rope with long, cautious pulls, mindful of the dangers of an electrical storm.

Even so, it was not over. We scrabbled down the boulder field, awkward with our rucksacks and the rain-soaked ropes, slipping on the slick stone and wincing as the ground shook and the Tower took direct lightning strikes.

By the time we got to the footpath, the bulk of the brief summer storm had passed us. Soaked through and battered, we trudged down to the visitors' center and signed out on the climbing roster. I handed it to a uniformed clerk who said, "Blown off, huh? Well—you got a late start. We tend to get weather in the afternoon this time of year."

Blown off. That was my consolation—the excuse handed me by a merciful God who knew as well as I did that, storm or no storm, there was no way I could have made it up the second pitch of the Durrance Route that afternoon. Middling rating or not, it was more route than I was climber. It ate at me that evening as we attended a naturalist's campfire lecture, ate at me the next morning as we packed the little Chevrolet for the long, dismal drive back East.

By the time we'd gotten home, I was convicted. I was going to go back, I was going to climb Devils Tower . . . and I was going to do it within a year.

My readiness program would consist of two parts.

The first was daily and regular exercise, aimed at gaining both strength and endurance. I avoided the use of a car, trying instead to bicycle to my classes (I was in graduate school at the time), and spent long hours in the university's gym, lifting weights and stretching to maintain flexibility. During an early summer canoe trip in Ontario's Algonquin Provincial Park, I delighted my companions by single-handedly portaging most of our canoes—at a brisk trot—over the quarter-mile to half-mile distances between lakes.

The other part of the program was climbing—climbing everything and anything that I could find. The climbable rock nearest to my home in those days was a stretch of cliff at Whipp's Ledges, in a metropark south of Cleveland, some one and a half hours away by car. I visited it once and sometimes twice a week, filling in the intervening days with climbs on the buildings at the University of Toledo—an activity requiring friends on the campus police department, so I would not be mistaken for a cat-burglar.

Slowly, as the months passed, the hard work paid off. My weight dropped from nearly 200 pounds to less than 167. I developed the ability to do ten pull-ups on any single finger of either hand and to crunch out conventional pull-ups and situps for minutes on end. Bruce Groves, an instructor in the parks-and-recreation program at the university, asked me to help him in his rock-climbing classes; once, while doing that, I hung by one hand from an overhang as I delivered a five-minute talk (one of the students timed it) on technique and strength conservation. Then, having finished the impromptu "lecture," I smoothly pulled myself to chin-level with one hand and finished the climb ropeless, going up and over the projecting rock. It was braggadocio, pure and simple, and I was loving it.

It's tempting now to say that I was young and foolish, but that wasn't it at all. Self-pride is self-pride, whatever age one is, and it is all too often a leash about one's neck, tugging insistently toward wreckage and ruin. In my case, it was leading toward a spiritual slap to the side of the head.

I kept working, honing the art of "friction" climbing, using balance and stealth to scale walls that lacked overt ledges or handholds, relying for my purchase on the tenuous friction of hands and feet against slight irregularities in the rock.

By the beginning of the following summer, I felt absolutely invincible, so confident of my ability to scale Devils Tower that I accepted an assignment to do a magazine article on the climb.

To get the pictures that would accompany the article, we planned to use five climbers. Three would go up the Durrance Route and act as photo models; the other two would climb an adjacent crack and shoot the climbers in profile for dramatic, airy images of the event.

Greg was away at school at the time, so I drove out to Wyoming with Rick Tapia, another longtime climbing partner. Slight in build and a marathon runner, Rick was the best crack-climber I knew, so adept at his craft that we'd nicknamed him "Spider Man."

When Rick and I arrived at the National Monument, it was after ten in the evening; the Park Service had closed and locked the gate for the night. We drove back up the road a mile or so, found a meadow that was relatively flat, and threw our sleeping bags there. I remember that it was mid-August, the time of the annual Pleiades meteor shower, and we marveled at the spectacle for hours on end, until fatigue finally coaxed us into sleep.

Sunrise awoke us early, so we drove into the National Monument campground, found a site, and pitched our tent. Then, because the day was still young, we took the car to the parking lot nearest the Tower, signed in with the Park Service, grabbed a pair of ropes and the equipment slings, and walked up the path to the base of the rock, intending to try only a pitch or two and familiarize ourselves with the lower portion of the climb.

27

Rick led the initial pitch; I wanted to lead the crux—the most difficult pitch of the climb—which followed. I remember the casual way he climbed, wasting not an iota of energy, his bandanna tied up in a cap, pirate-fashion, to keep the small rocks and debris out of his hair. He finished off in short order and I started up to join him, the pitch much easier than I'd found it the year before. When I joined him on the ledge, I lingered only long enough to transfer some of the larger chocks from Rick's equipment sling to mine. Then I was climbing again, moving up the crux pitch.

For the first fifteen or twenty feet, I stemmed from crack to crack, as I had the year before. Then, when I reached the bulge, I jammed a fist into the right-hand crack and let my feet drop under me, moving smoothly past the obstacle in a series of one-handed pull-ups, not even bothering to place a protective chockstone as I climbed. Up I went, over the bulge and onto the easier ground above. When I called "Belay off," Rick answered back from 120 feet below: "I don't have to do it *exactly* that way, do I?"

Only two pitches up, we were already on top of the world. The climb, which had seemed so overwhelming just a year before, was almost laughably easy. Rick joined me, and we did the rest of the climb in tandem. I led, put in a couple of protection points, and Rick followed, the two of us climbing simultaneously with the rope strung between us. We got to The Meadows, crossed the ledge, followed an easy crack to the top, put our signatures in the notebook inside the .30-caliber ammunition box that served as a summit register, and then did the three rappels needed to get back down. Along the way, we tarried a moment to retrieve another party's climbing rope that had become stuck on the lower rappel. Even so, our time for the ascent and descent (normally a five-hour endeavor), was less than two hours.

Bruce Groves had arrived at the base of the Tower as Rick and I were topping out, bringing with him a virtual man-mountain named C. H. Burnett—a plumber by trade, with exceptional upper body strength and a viselike grip. We were flushed with excitement as they met us at the trailhead.

"It's cake," we told them. "A piece of cake; no problems at all."

Actually, there was one problem. Our fifth man was hors de combat, a sprained ankle rendering him unable to climb. To ask one man to climb solo was out of the question, so we quickly came up with an alternate strategy.

Bruce, Rick, and I would take turns leading the climb, bringing C. H. up as a second. Then, at the top of each rope-pitch, we would lower C. H. off and allow him to pendulum over to an adjacent crack, anchor in, and un-rope. The leader would then rappel back down the pitch, and the climb would be repeated for the camera.

Doing things this way meant that the leaders of each pitch would, in effect, be climbing the Tower twice, as would C. H., and we would incur the additional penalty of having to fix a camera position several times as we made the ascent. There being no other means available for us to get the photography I needed, we conceded that we would be in for a very long day of rock-climbing, indeed.

The approach was still damp with dew the next morning as the four of us scrambled up the boulder field to the bottom of the climb.

The climb was as time-consuming as we'd expected, the work grueling as the sun heated the rock face. We emptied most of our water bottles in short order and then climbed thirsty, determined to summit for the benefit of the cameras and saving the last bottle for a sip on top.

By the time we got to The Meadows, it was already quite late in the afternoon. Our route, which had taken just two hours the day before, now looked as if it would require every bit of ten. To save time, I proposed doing the last pitch, from The Meadows to the top of the Tower, rope-less. It had been easy ground the day before, and we saw little danger in dispensing with the protection of the ropes if it could shave a few minutes.

There was only one drawback to this plan. From our perspective at the end of The Meadows, several of the cracks looked the same, and we weren't certain which we had followed to the top the day before. Two of them appeared promising, but both lines leaned inward in their upper reaches, preventing us from seeing anything but the lower portions of each route.

To me, the right-hand line appeared the most familiar. It consisted, as did the other, of two cracks with a pillar inset between them; a classic "chimney."

"This is it," I told the others. Then I added, "At least . . . I'm pretty sure it is. Maybe I'd better run up first, just to check."

As if in celestial response, the sky darkened. Clouds were rolling in over the top of the Tower. Looking off into the distance, we could see a suddenly mottled landscape—patches of sunlight alternating with the dark shadows of cloud.

"Are you sure you don't want a rope?" Bruce asked.

I looked at the sky and then shook my head, not wanting to cede any time to the approaching weather.

"I'll just carry it up," I told him, stowing the fifty-meter climbing line in my rucksack. Certain rain was on the way, I wanted to get up top, take a picture for the magazine, and get down as quickly as possible. After a year of training, I couldn't picture any circumstance that could stop me. "When I know for sure where this route goes, I'll call down and you can follow. Let's finish her off."

The wind was rippling my shirt as I started up. The basalt surface of the opposing columns was still warm from the vanquished sun as I nestled my back and hands against one side and pushed with my smooth-rubber climbing shoes against the other. By alternately inching first my back and then my feet upwards, I could make steady progress. The two columns were leaning slightly toward one another, so I had to keep a constant pressure against them to prevent myself from sliding down, but in all the climbing was easy. In a matter of a minute or so, I was forty feet above the ledge and moving smoothly. I felt comfortable, pleased that the year of hard work had readied me for this climb.

The route curved gradually inward. Ten yards farther, I lost sight of my companions and the ledge on which they stood. Looking down, all I could see was the boulder field eight hundred feet below, the green fir bristles of treetops, and then, curving grayly under the growing cloud, the Platte River, now nearly eleven hundred feet beneath my feet.

The wind picked up again as I leaned out in an attempt to see the upper reaches of my route. My heart sank. The chimney didn't run unobstructed all the way to the top. About thirty feet above me, a remnant of a basalt column was lodged across the top of my chimney, blocking my way.

The wind positively whipped at my shirt as I considered the options. Unroped, attempting to climb over the overhanging obstacle was virtually unthinkable. I could go down or hope to find a path to either side.

After three hails to the group below, I got a reply and yelled, "This isn't the route! Use the other!"

"You all righ– . . . ?" came the partial reply between gusts of wind.

Was I? My earlier confidence was ebbing, but I still had complete faith in my ability to climb and work the problems out using my own resources.

"I'm okay!" I shouted in reply. "I'll find a way around this and see you up top."

"Oka–, see you on to– . . ." came the tattered reply, ripped by the gusting wind.

I looked again at the obstacle above me. As I did, it began to rain.

Had I roped up for this pitch, I could have put in a chock, clipped in with a carabiner, and let my partners lower me off the pitch. But to even try to remove the rope from my rucksack would have meant risking a slip and an unarrested fall to the ledge or possibly even the boulder field below.

Nor could I easily back down. The chimney was what climbers call a "Bombay chimney," meaning that it was wider at the bottom than it was at the top. While upward progress comes fairly easily in such a chimney, going back down would again risk a slip and a fall, particularly with the surfaces turning slick with rain.

So I climbed up, as far as I could, until I was just under the hanging pillar. There, partly shielded from the now-steady drizzle, I inspected the cracks to either side and found them to be knife-thin. Even if I wished to risk going up and over the hanging rock, the cracks were not wide enough to afford me purchase.

"Piece 'a cake. . . . No problem at all. . . . Maybe I'd better run up first."

My words were coming back to haunt me. Precious minutes slipped by. Perched tenuously under the overhanging pillar, my legs were already beginning to tremble from the effort of holding myself in place on the rain-slick rock. By now, I figured, Rick, Bruce, and C. H. were well into their final pitch to the summit. Even assuming that they might hear a call for help in the rising wind, it would consume at least half an hour for them to get back down to The Meadows and then bring a rope and rappelling hardware up to me—and down-climbing even an easy pitch could be hazardous in the rain.

Next, I mentally calculated how long it would take my companions to climb to the top of the Tower, realize I was in trouble, and lower a rope to me. Could I maintain my position long enough for them to do that? I doubted it. Staying put in a chimney for too long inevitably resulted in "sewing-machine legs"—muscle spasms from the prolonged exertion. I knew that the summer showers in this part of the country often ended in minutes, but I also knew that I would probably slip from my perch long before the wind dried the rock. I looked again at the ceiling of rock above me, then out at the rain- and cloud-shrouded landscape, and I regretted my cavalier attitude.

I couldn't go up, couldn't go down. I was well and truly stuck.

Or was I? Just below my eye level, the far pillar—the one against my feet—was cracked, the upper part of the rock inset a scant half inch from the lower portion. It formed the thinnest of ledges, not enough to stand on securely, but enough, if one formed a half-fist, to gain a slender purchase with the fingertips.

The rain was increasing. My friction boots' smooth rubber bottoms would stick like glue to a clean, dry rock surface, but were practically worthless on the wet. And the rock certainly wasn't getting any drier. Waiting could only make matters worse.

Moving one foot behind me, I pressed, like a hurdler, using the opposing pressure of my feet to "stand" my upper body between the two rock walls. Wiping my damp hands against my shirt, I hung my fingertips on the thin but distinct little ledge, and then, as carefully as I could, I relaxed the pressure of my feet.

Much too abruptly, my boots slipped off the rock, leaving my legs dangling beneath me. But the hands held; I was now literally suspended by my fingertips.

Half-chinning myself, I walked my feet up the wall beneath me and began to crab sideways, out of the chimney and around the far pillar. The wind was insistent now, the rain a steady drizzle.

A thin film of water was sheeting down the rock, trickling over the ledge and my clenched fingers. Cold rain peppered my eyes every time I looked up.

The column was approximately seven feet wide; before I'd gotten halfway across, my feet had slipped out from under me twice. I hung by my nails, more than eight hundred feet up a pillar of rock; the distant boulder field dim and veiled through the misting rain.

Climbers refer to the feeling of air beneath one's feet as "exposure," and I was experiencing it in spades, fantastically perched on a vertical wall with the elements seeking to evict me. To fall was unthinkable, yet distinctly possible.

In practice, rock climbers often use a technique called "bouldering," rehearsing difficult moves on cliff faces or boulders just a few feet, or even inches, off the ground. The idea is to hone skills in an environment in which one can fall safely, long before those skills are used on an actual climb. To steel my nerves, I imagined myself in such an exercise. It was the equivalent of walking across a wooden beam lying flat on the ground, as opposed to walking across the same beam suspended between two buildings; in the former case, a mistake would be quite unlikely, although in the latter it could well be catastrophic.

One inch. Six inches. One foot. As I crabbed along the delicate traverse, my world shrank to a small oval of rain-wet basalt around me. Outer concerns, larger thoughts of the world, vanished as I focused in, concentrated on finding the next handhold and keeping my feet against the rock.

Minutes later, the vertical crack on the far side of the pillar was tantalizingly close. It was wide and open, and even with a small cataract of water sheeting down it, it looked infinitely preferable to where I was. I was half-tempted to lunge, but I resisted as I remembered missing the "bucket" hold in West Virginia the year before. Fingers white and numb with the effort, I inched closer, reached out with my left foot and wiggled my boot toe into the crack, and then, holding on with my right hand, I reached out with my left and caught the crack.

There. I was there. I got the other boot into the crack and then released the little ledge, flexing my numbed right hand to drive the blood back into it. It came achingly back to life, then I switched hands, did the same with the left, and took my first full, deep breaths in several minutes.

All things considered, I was still quite exposed, hanging by my fists and boot tips to a damp crack more than eight hundred feet up a wind- and rain-swept rock. But in comparison to where I had been, the new stance felt like a platform. I leaned back on my handholds and inspected the route above. The crack ran, wide and true, all the way up; I could see bits of prairie grass growing from the weathered rock on top.

The drizzle gradually diminished as I made my way, climbing methodically, like a machine, to the broad, sloping summit plateau. As I moved onto the easy ground at the top, I grabbed a small cactus by mistake and didn't even care: it was too good just to be alive. Dampened and exhausted, I set foot onto the top; my companions, be-panchoed and worried, bustling over to greet me.

"How was it?" Rick asked.

I took a step forward and my knees buckled, nearly spilling me onto the ground.

"That bad, huh?" Bruce commented as he caught me by the arm.

C. H. unstoppered the water bottle and offered me a drink, but I smiled and shook my head. I was on top of the world—and I'd had quite my fill of water.

Proverbs 11:2 teaches us that pride brings shame. But the same Scripture adds that humility is often accompanied by wisdom.

There are at least two ways in which pride can lead us into danger.

The first is when pride leads us to overestimate or overstate our abilities. At the time we climbed Long's Peak, neither Greg nor I had the skills to mount a rescue on the Diamond Direct route. Had we actually made the attempt, we would have done so at peril to both ourselves and the person we were trying to save.

The second way our pride ensnares us is when we deliberately underestimate the challenges we face. During our first attempt on Devils Tower, my partner and I underestimated it and as a result failed to complete the climb. I then knew it deserved respect, yet, on my return, I insisted on again belittling the challenge and nearly paid the ultimate penalty for my imprudence.

Simple logic dictates that pride is much more common than it should be. There are few things less likeable than an arrogant boaster and few qualities more attractive than silent humility. Yet the former is far more prevalent than the latter. Perhaps this is because quiet people—those who allow others to spread word of their accomplishments—become known over time, by degrees, and we live in an age that prefers the instantaneous. Perhaps prudence—the reasoned caution of a wise person—is too often mistaken for cowardice. Whatever the reason, a larger-than-life reputation is one commodity that has always been in fierce demand.

After all, we live in a world that encourages pride. When I was in school, I recall that I was nearly constantly reminded of my pride as a justification and a reason for excelling in scholastics, or sports, or extracurricular activities. "Pride" became synonymous in the public vernacular with "self-respect" or "depend-

ability"—two very laudable traits—and lost its more precise association with "vanity" and "egotism." When that happened, pride lost its sting, and that was regrettable, because the fact of the matter is that God—the ultimate Judge of every human being—hates pride, despises it, and is rightly displeased with us when we exhibit it.

In Mark 7:22, Jesus Himself lists pride among the most inherently evil of human sins, including it with such acts as adultery, fornication, murder, theft, and blasphemy.

Our Lord does so with good reason, as pride is the source of most—and possibly all—human sin. When Eve succumbed to the serpent's temptation, it was her pride that was working on her, kindling the desire to be on an equal footing with God. When Adam joined her, he did so because he was too proud to show the fear and hesitation that his Creator had rightly placed within his heart. And later, when God accepted the blood offering of Abel over the grain offering of Cain, that perceived slight wounded Cain's pride to such an extent that he rose up in anger and took the life of his own brother.

In Exodus 17:6, God enabled Moses to create a spring of water for the children of Israel in Horeb by striking a rock with his staff. Later, in the desert of Zin, when the people again needed water, God told Moses to simply speak (Numbers 20:8) to a rock to create another spring. But as Numbers 20:10–12 records, Moses was not content to simply obey God's word. Rather than speaking to the rock, he addressed the people, saying, "Hear now . . . rebels; must we fetch you water out of this rock?" And having said that, he struck the rock with his staff, creating the illusion that it was he, and not God, who miraculously provided the water. And, for this transgression, God refused to allow Moses to enter the promised land of Canaan—the destination for which they were crossing the desert in the first place.

Anger is a weapon forged from pride; fear and worry are the shields the prideful man raises to defend his frail self-image. Self-congratulation and bragging come naturally to man, but they do so at great cost, since all that is good and worthy proceeds directly *from God, and for man to claim the credit is nothing more than an absolute fraud.*

Pride is, in short, the corrosive and corruptive element that leads us to rely upon and elevate our imperfect selves, rather than to submit to and follow the will of our perfect heavenly Father.

When a Christian chooses to follow his pride, he also follows a path away from the Holy Spirit, the God-given and godly "Comforter" that Jesus promised to each Christian in John 14:16.

When I was making the climbs described in this narrative, I had not yet realized Jesus Christ as my personal Savior, so I was dealing with very high stakes, indeed. A fall for a saved person—a Christian—may have meant being crippled or even being killed, but it would not have changed the ultimate outcome; it could not have kept that person from heaven. But to fall to one's death on the boulder field below would have meant the ultimate tragedy for a lost—or unsaved—person, since that fall would have ended in hell . . . an eternal separation from God and an eternal punishment for a lifetime of sin.

To successfully climb Devils Tower, I trained relentlessly for a full year. I exercised to gain both strength and endurance and practiced by climbing everything in sight.

Were I making the same climb today, I would still go into intensive physical training, and I would still practice-climb extensively. But I would also add a third element to my preparations—an element more important than either of the others—and that would be prayer.

Nor would my prayers be a simple request for success. I would begin by thanking God for His myriad blessings, and then I would ask Him to show me His will in all matters—including whether or not I should even be making such a climb—and to grant me the humility and obedience necessary to recognize His will.

As Christians, we carry the power of God within us constantly in the form of the Holy Spirit, but as men, we also carry carnal desires for self-glorification (fueled by a very real Devil who would

38

*like to see us become slaves to those desires). As God's beloved cre-
ations, we possess the free will to choose between the two.*

*There is only one way to prevent pride from staining or ruin-
ing us, and that is to admit that we are powerless to overcome it—
or any other sin—and accept the only One who can save us from
it: Jesus Christ.*

*This, in itself, is an act of humility. It is an acknowledgment
of the very real fact that we can't go it alone, that we must rely
upon another—God the Son—to pay our sin-debt for us.*

*Once we have done that, we need to be watchful for signs of
pride in our lives.*

*When someone praises our accomplishments, do we simply
thank them for the compliment and move on (the polite thing to
do), or do we milk the situation for all it's worth?*

*When we are asked to do something for which we haven't the
talent, or to answer a question beyond our knowledge, do we have
the humility to say, "I am not able," or "I don't know," or do we
try to bolster our self-esteem by bluffing?*

*When someone else does well, do we have the courage to con-
gratulate, or do we sulk and nurse our wounded pride?*

*When the Holy Spirit is exhorting us—when right cries out to
be done—do we do it, even if it is not the popular action, or do
we save face by sticking with the crowd?*

*When we see signs of pride, we need to confess the sin—for
pride is a sin—and ask Jesus for His help in avoiding that sin in
the future.*

*Proverbs 16:18 is often paraphrased as "pride comes before a
fall." As I nearly discovered on Devils Tower, that admonition
should sometimes be taken literally.*

*Two good tools to use in avoiding pride are to look for oppor-
tunities to applaud or give credit to others and, when others
applaud us, to dwell on it as little as possible or, better still, to gen-
uinely and wholeheartedly give the glory to its rightful Author—
God. Oddly enough, such humility actually accomplishes the thing
that people try, and fail, to accomplish with bragging and self-
promotion; it tends to make people like and respect us. Proverbs*

22:4 nails it right on the head: "By humility and the fear of the Lord are riches, and honor, and life."

As with every word of God, this is very, very true. And one of the greatest riches of all is knowing that you are depending on a perfect and supernatural Power—and giving the credit only where the credit is due.

2

INTO THE
DEVIL'S EAR

*They meet with darkness in the daytime,
and grope in the noonday as in the night.*
JOB 5:14

Mention "Florida" to virtually anyone and, chances are,
you'll conjure up a specific image. To some, Florida is sun,
white sand, and beaches. To others, Florida is the great salt
ocean and a day at sea, backing down in a frothing wake
on a shimmering marlin. Golfers see Florida as manicured
courses and palm-fringed greens, and the fashion-con-
scious restrict their vision to a few square miles of Miami.
For many youngsters, Florida is a world of fairy-tale theme
parks—fantasy kingdoms that have fireworks every night.

But for me, the best part of Florida is in the north. This
is Brahman cattle-farm country, sandy-soiled flatland
punctuated by pulp pine being grown for the paper mills

and live oaks draped in sleepy Spanish moss. Oddly enough, northern Florida is the only part of the state that is truly Southern in character, the lower portion of the peninsula being populated primarily by Yankees escaping the Snowbelt. Here, people drawl languidly when they speak, have hominy grits for breakfast, move at a measured pace appropriate to the rural heat, and exhibit a level of gentility their northern cousins have not known for decades.

North central Florida is also the region of the state that is richest in freshwater springs. In some areas, these springs are "blue holes"—so named because they issue a continual torrent of exceptionally clear, turquoise-tinted water. The clarity and color give these apertures the appearance of azure, otherworldly portals.

In other areas, the only sign one might see of a spring is a cauldron-like disturbance in the center of a pond or a clear strip of water streaking down a swatch of tea-brown, tannin-tinted river.

Clear water is the hallmark of a classic Florida spring, and it is this water clarity that has fed what tourist industry there is in the region. Miami- or Orlando-bound vacationers will often stop for a day or two to take in a glass-bottom boat tour or an underwater ballet performed by tail-finned "mermaids."

My preference, though, is to see the springs from the other side—from within the underwater caves that feed the flow of the beautiful blue holes.

I am a cave diver. Cave divers make their way through mazelike, totally flooded passages, forever out of the reach of sunlight. They find their way with fragile, battery-powered lights and breathe from steadily diminishing cylinders of compressed gas. They swim, pull, push, and wriggle through situations that would be a claustrophobe's worst nightmare. The slightest disturbance will often waft up centuries' worth of sediment, reducing visibility to zero in the twinkling of an eye. Cave diving is an activity that comes, in most people's estimation, about as close to perdition as one is likely to get on this side of the grave. And yet, cave divers pursue their activity willingly, finding it recreational, enjoyable, highly satisfying—even peaceful.

To understand the attraction these North Florida caves hold on those who dive them, I would take you back to a late spring morning when three companions and I took a trip into the main cave passage at the Devil's Ear, a high-volume spring on the edge of the Santa Fe River.

Located near and connected underground to a circular spring opening known as the Devil's Eye, the entrance to the Devil's Ear is a daunting phone-booth-size opening from which water gushes at seemingly fire-hydrant velocity. Swimming into such an opening is next to impossible; it is all one can do to duck down to a lower edge and pull oneself through. But once past the entrance, the passage opens up enormously, and a large entry cavern leads to a mostly horizontal passage, spacious enough to accommodate a submerged semi-trailer.

On this particular dive, I was the last man in, following easily behind my friends. As we made our way through the clear water, we communicated with one another by shining our dive-lights on the water-sculpted walls of the passage. A circle traced with the light indicated that all was well. Moving it side to side was the signal for "danger." Bobbing a light up and down was a call for attention.

At length, near an extremely low section of the cave known as "The Lips," our leader bobbed his beam three times in succession on the wall ahead of us. He held up his pressure gauge and three fingers, then changed to thumbs-up, indicating that he had depleted a third of his air supply and was ready to turn the dive and head back toward the surface.

The business with the gauge was an unnecessary courtesy. An inviolable code of cave diving holds that any diver can "call" any dive at any time, with no explanation called for and no questions afterward. But, in most cave diving, one third of the breathing supply is used for entry, another third is used for the exit, and the remaining third is held in reserve for emergencies. By showing us that he was adhering to this "thirds" rule, our leader removed any doubt as to the reason for the exit and helped keep our party collected and at ease.

Another rule of cave diving is maintenance of the order-of-file. As last diver in, I would automatically become the first diver out, leading our group back to the headpool from which we'd begun.

With my dive-light, I painted a large circle on the passage wall—cavers' shorthand for "okay"—and then raised my own thumb to indicate that I'd correctly received the signal. I turned and began to take our group down the dark route back to daylight.

On the way in, we had been traveling against the flow, gentle as it was in the large passage, kicking to make progress upstream.

But on the exit, the flow assisted us. I hovered in the middle of the passage, absolutely neutral—neither sinking nor rising—and allowed the water to carry me gently back along our route. It was the most effortless form of travel imaginable, like the flight one enjoys in dreams, needing neither movement nor exertion, only the thought and the desire to sail along. In moments, my breathing had subsided to a deeply relaxed minimum. I bent my knees and kept my fins slightly above me, well clear of the sleeping silt on the floor. The dive-light in my hand felt nearly weightless. The heavy steel tanks were only a faint presence on my shoulders and my back; astronauts in space are scarcely more free from gravity than a neutrally buoyant diver. I floated on in the penumbra from our lights, the cave-flow carrying me effortlessly along a bend in the broad, wide passage.

Going in, I'd both felt and heard the current pushing past my neoprene-hooded head. Coming out, I could hear nothing but the rush of our exhaust bubbles, racing along the pocked, stone ceiling.

Drifting effortlessly, lazily, I marveled at the clarity of the water. Our group had been careful going in, and it showed—not a speck of silt sullied the crystal-clear water. The visibility easily exceeded two hundred feet, better than one would expect in the clearest of swimming pools. As I drifted, I bent downward, tucked my chin against my chest, and looked back, upside-down, at the team behind me.

The water, although clear, had hue, a delicate blue that deepened with distance. My companions were all holding their lights before their chests, their bodies outlined dimly by the backwash from the lamps. And the lights, at that distance, were the color of purest topaz. I gazed for a long time at the divers who followed me, the three of them drifting without effort down the middle of the broad passage, heavenly blue orbs of light gleaming exactly in the vicinity of their hearts.

That image stays with me still. It was beautiful, unearthly—the very likeness, I imagine, of angels.

Unfortunately, it is this great beauty, and the extraordinary clarity of the spring waters, that is cave-country's greatest curse. From the entrance of a cave, it appears one can see forever, and the gentle push of the outflow seems certain to bring any who enter back into the daylight. Lulled by this tranquil beauty, unschooled divers sometimes wander into caves, totally unaware that their undulating fins are churning up great, thick clouds of powdery clay and sediment behind them. This matter can remain suspended for an hour or more at a time, creating a dense and impenetrable "silt-out" that robs the diver of all visibility.

Divers have panicked and drowned in such conditions, only a dozen feet from a cave entrance and the open water above. Even a simple and straightforward cave can reap its share of unwary explorers. Although educational campaigns and warning signs have now slowed the accident rate in cave diving to an isolated mishap or two over the whole of Florida each year, cave divers train rigorously to keep themselves and their companions safe.

A basic premise of this training is that equipment failure and other mishaps are statistically inevitable. Eventually, over hundreds or thousands of dives, lights will fail, no matter how rigorously they are checked before the dive begins. Even the best of regulators—the hose-and-mouthpiece devices that deliver divers their air—will sometimes free-flow, sticking open and emptying a tank of all of its air.

To deal with such contingencies, the cave diver assumes that they will happen, and each dive is planned in full cognizance of Murphy's Law. To safeguard themselves in the event of light failures, all cave divers carry at least three lights—one to dive with and two as backups with which to exit, in the event that the primary light fails.

Since regulators are mechanical devices, and any mechanical device can malfunction, cave divers use at least two regulators. Each one is governed by its own, independent valve, generally on a manifold leading to two high-capacity scuba tanks. In the event that one regulator fails, the valve leading to it is shut off, and the diver exits using the other regulator, which can draw air from either tank or both.

Even total loss of visibility is accepted as a "given" by the cave diver. Divers enter the water carrying at least two reels, each holding a healthy supply of guideline. One of these reels is generally used as a primary reel, to mark a trail from open water to the permanent guideline (which usually begins twenty or thirty feet into the cave). The other reel is kept for emergencies. In caves in which permanent guideline has not been laid, an exploration reel—larger and carrying more line that the typical reel—is used by the lead diver to lay a line. And small reels known as "gap reels" are used to create a bridge when divers move from one permanent guideline to another. The business with line reels is important, since the first rule of cave diving is to maintain a continuous guideline back to open water at all times. All divers stay near to, and in sight of, the line throughout their dive. Should the lights fail or a silt-out occur, divers go to the guideline, make contact with it, and follow it—by sense of touch—back to safety.

Since the guideline is so vital to the diver's safety, proper equipment is essential. The guideline used in cave diving is a triple-braided nylon line, extremely resistant to abrasion, and absolutely impervious to rot. Cave divers train with this equipment to the point that visibility becomes a luxury rather than a necessity. Line-reel drills and the use of touch-communication enable dive teams to proceed under conditions in which it is literally impossible to see anything at all.

My own trial-by-fire in this discipline came the day before my dive in the Devil's Ear, in a system known as Little River Cave, near Branford, Florida.

The Little River is just that—a stream that issues from a freshwater headspring and runs a scant two hundred yards before emptying itself into the tannin-stained waters of the Itchetucknee River.

But the cave that lies beneath that spring is massive and complex, running in an ant-colony-like maze under miles of the north-Florida countryside.

Dustin Clesi, a former stockbroker who "retired" in his thirties to pursue a career teaching cave diving, brought another student and me to Little River just a few minutes before sundown. We suited up on the tailgate of Dustin's truck, made our way down the rickety wooden stairway leading to the spring basin, and did our briefing standing chest-deep in the clear, seventy-two-degree water. Dustin called "one minute," and we zeroed our dive watches and stood silently, collecting our thoughts and calming our breathing. Sixty seconds later, Dustin signaled thumbs-down, and we all slipped noiselessly into the steadily out-flowing water.

Lights on, we glided through the broad entrance aperture, over a tablelike shelf, and down a steep stone ramp, ducking under the overhanging ceiling and stopping, nearly sixty feet underwater, to tie off Dustin's guideline on a large stone block.

With Dustin in the lead, we made our way along the curving, downsloping, tubelike passage. Occasionally, Dustin stopped to wrap the line around an outcropping and keep it oriented near the center of the passage. Sometimes, he simply picked up a platter-size rock and placed it atop the line to keep it taunt and running straight.

We swam deep into the blackness of the Little River entrance passage. Finally, just above a steep chimney that plummeted straight down into the bowels of the cave, we arrived at a wide spot and Dustin raised a clinched fist: cave-diver's sign language for "hold." He pointed to our lights and, per his previous instructions, my partner and I did something we would never have even considered under normal conditions: We switched them off.

Dustin extinguished his own fifty-watt primary light, leaving just one small back-up lamp burning. He raised a hand in the "OK" sign and, circling the line with my other hand, I returned it. Looking me in the eyes, Dustin nodded. After one final inspection to see that all was in readiness, he turned the last light off.

In the twinkling of an eye it became dark. It became darker than dark. The loss of light was absolute, complete, as if I had suddenly been struck blind. Sounds—the prolonged gurgle of the regulators, the rusk of air bubbles along the rocky ceiling, the disturbance of the current flowing past us, the occasional ring of steel tanks against stone—still surrounded me but were sourceless in the all-encompassing blackness.

The purpose of this dive was to test my ability to get my partner and myself out of the cave without the assistance of light. I'd been trained for this contingency. I was ready for it. But even so, I was not prepared for the sudden change in my environment.

I raised a gauge and looked at the luminous dial to assure myself that I could actually still see. The dim dial of the radium face glowed a ghostly green in the darkness, but my eyesight, while still intact, was of no use whatsoever. Without a dive-light to pierce the blackness, there simply was nothing to look at.

The outflow nudged us insistently. It reminded me that, with each breath we took, the supply of air in our tanks was diminishing, had been diminishing since we started the dive. It was time to move.

I had trained in the use of a guideline. I'd run drills—first on dry land and then in open water with my eyes closed. But this was different. Eyes open or eyes closed, it made no difference. For all intents and purposes, I was blind. My partner pushed against the calf of my leg—ready to move. Raising my free arm to block and fend off obstructions, I began to swim carefully, letting the current push me down the passage.

Because touch is so important in a lightless environment, most cave divers generally wear either fingerless mitts or no gloves at all. I had opted for the latter, giving me as much sensitivity as possible. The idea was to keep the guideline running loosely through my encircling fingers. Pressure of the line on my thumb would mean I was moving too far to the right; pressure on the index finger would indicate that I was drifting too far left. Similarly, as the passage crossed depressions or went over ramps, pressure on the line would allow me to know if I was swimming too high or too low. Touch communications—one squeeze for "stop," two squeezes for "hold," a push for "go"—allowed my partner to communicate with me.

As we felt our way along the passage, I began to get the impression, almost the certainty, that I could somehow see in the dark. Ahead of me, in the darkness, I sensed a vaguely deeper blackness—the passage?

I swam toward it and was rewarded with a resounding thump in the head. I had swum into solid rock. The "passage" I'd thought I'd seen was nothing more than an illusion. Deprived of visual input, my mind was inventing its own images. I ignored them and concentrated on following the guideline.

I bumped my tanks against the ceiling and descended, barely hovering above the floor of the passage. Moving on, I bumped my tanks again. A few feet farther, the floor and ceiling had pinched down to a point that my chest was on the floor and my tanks were rubbing the ceiling. I tried squirming, but things just got tighter.

Fully aware that, as the seconds passed, my partner and I were steadily breathing away the air within our tanks, I stopped to think the situation through.

It was, I knew, simply a drill. My lights, although extinguished, were still with me, clipped off on my dive harness. All I had to do was turn one on and I would instantly be able to diagnose my problem. I considered doing just that but, had I done so, I would have failed the exercise. Besides, the guideline assured me that we had somehow come in this way—and since we'd been able to get in, we would be able to get out.

Still retaining my contact with the line, I felt the rock around me with my free hand, followed it, and felt it sloping up and away.

In a matter of seconds, I had a picture of what had happened. I'd simply moved the guideline over into a "line trap"—a low area to the side of the passage. I felt my way around the obstacle and continued moving up the passage, the guideline feeding smoothly through my hand, my partner still in contact with me, following along like a vessel in tow. We breathed easily, knowing we were headed for the sweet, open air beyond.

Ten minutes later, I saw—actually saw—a vague oval of dim, blue luminescence. It was twilight filtering through the cave entrance. We'd made it.

Behind us, a dive-lamp came on. It was Dustin, who'd been following behind us, touching our tanks to keep track of us and timing his breathing so the sounds of his regulator blended with that of our own. Unbeknownst to us, he'd been with us, all the way.

More dives would soon follow—in the crystal waters of Devil's Ear, throughout the Peacock Springs cave system, in other, more remote springs around the state. But they would be easier with the knowledge that, even in total darkness, I could still find my way home.

And knowing that, the darkness would never again seem as deep.

"And thou shalt grope at noonday," says Deuteronomy 28:29, "as the blind gropeth in darkness, and thou shalt not prosper in thy ways: and thou shalt be only oppressed and spoiled evermore, and no man shall save thee."

The very idea of cave diving—of going into a deep and maze-like underwater passage, devoid of natural light, carrying only the number of breaths one can pump into a scuba tank—is foreign and even terrifying to most people.

"What if you lose your way?" The questions escalate. "What if your lights fail? What if you run out of air?"

The thing that amazes—and terrifies—me is that many of the people who ask these very questions are people who have never accepted Jesus Christ as their Savior. Some of these people have actually heard God's perfect plan of salvation and rejected it. Others cling to false methods—their own works, or mistaken beliefs— and think that those are the ways to heaven.

I ask you—who is in the greater peril? If I become hopelessly lost in a cave, I may lose my life. But these lost individuals are in a much more precarious predicament; unless they find Christ as their Savior, what is at peril for them is the state of their eternal soul.

Think about it. Is there really any difference between a diver who journeys in a pitch-dark, water-filled cave and every single one of us?

The diver's breaths are numbered—he has only what he carries in his tanks. Yet none of us has an unlimited number of breaths allotted to us. Just as the hairs of our heads are numbered, and God knows that number, so also are the number of breaths we will take in this life. God knows that number, as well.

The cave diver is in peril of losing his way. But life is much more complicated—has infinitely more twists, turns, dead-ends and cul-de-sacs—than any cave that has ever been explored.

Take away his light, and the cave diver will grope—he may even imagine that he sees a way where none is there. Deprived of spiritual light, we will grope, as well—and we think we see paths that will lead us out of the abyss, but those are only the deceptive inventions of our own imaginations.

In the end, there is no difference at all. We are all in the cave.

We are in, as Job 10:22 puts it, "A land of darkness, as darkness itself; and of the shadow of death, without any order, and where the light is as darkness."

In fact, Job 22:11 draws the cave-diving analogy even more exactly, "Or darkness . . . and abundance of waters cover thee."

But the dark world described in the Book of Job is far more sinister than the world beneath Florida's springs; it is the sin-fraught world in which every one of us lives. And like a water-filled cave, it can be very, very dangerous.

In just one of the caves in which I took my training, more than three dozen scuba divers have perished over the years. Most were not trained for this type of diving, and none were observing all of the rules that have been established for this extremely advanced pursuit.

Yet they found the dark world seductive. They went in, went on, went farther than they should have, and ultimately could not come back.

To many sin-scarred individuals, such a situation probably sounds all too familiar—too similar to what they've experienced in life.

During my drill in the Little River cave system, I had several factors in my favor. I had been readied for the situation; I had a guideline to follow; and I had (though I was not aware of it at the time) a capable guide, right there, with me, at all times.

To take me confidently through life, I also have several factors that are overwhelmingly in my favor:

1. I've been readied. *Matthew 18:11 assures us, "For the Son of man is come to save that which was lost." On one quiet but memorable February afternoon, sitting and talking with the man who would later become my pastor, I became a Christian; I accepted Christ as my Savior. Life lost its terror then. I understood that, no matter what would happen to me here on this earth, I was bound to spend eternity with my Savior in that perfect place He has prepared for me.*

It took many days of intensive training to ready me to dive in a water-filled cave. To ready me for God's forgiveness—for heaven—took only moments. All I had to do was realize that I was a sinner, repent (set my mind in opposition to a sin-led life and in favor of a Christ-led life), and understand and believe that

Jesus Christ paid for my sins when He went to the cross and offered Himself as a sacrifice in my place. Then, understanding this, I simply had to accept, of my own free will, the gift of eternal life that Jesus Christ had so graciously given to me.

It's important to note that this repentance, belief, and acceptance is not simply a logical decision, not something one makes in the mind (like accepting a job offer), but a spiritual decision one makes in the heart (like falling in love). In Acts 8:37, when the disciple Philip counsels an Ethiopian nobleman, and the nobleman asks whether he can make a profession of his faith, Philip replies, "If thou believest with all thine heart, thou mayest."

From this, we understand that heartfelt belief is a central part of our acceptance of God's great gift of Christian salvation.

I'll be frank; it is preferable—it will be better for you in life—if you accept Jesus as your Savior sooner, rather than later. Proverbs 22:6 teaches us, "Train up a child in the way he should go: and when he is old, he will not depart from it."

This is fine advice; the earlier you become a Christian, the more readily you will make Christian principles a part of your life. It's not something you want to wait on.

I need to point out here that, once I was certified as a cave diver, I was, needless to say, hardly an expert. All I had were the minimal skills. But countless dives would hone my abilities, and I am still honing them today.

It's the same way with my Christian life: Salvation made me a Christian and "certified" me as a brother in Christ, but I would need to grow spiritually—making a profession of my faith, being obedient to God's will and sharing the gospel with others—in order to become a mature Christian. This, too, is an ongoing process; I grow more as a Christian every day.

__2. I have a guideline.__ God provided for my salvation. He also provided a guideline—instructions written in His own words—for me to use as I progress through life. That guideline is God's own Book, the Holy Bible.

Just as the genuine guideline used in cave diving is an essential piece of equipment, the holy Book I use in life must also be genuine.

A cave-diving guideline made of soluble material, or braided in a fashion that could cause it to unravel, would be worse than no guideline at all, since it would create a sense of confidence grounded on a fraud. In the same manner, a "holy book" espousing any path to heaven other than that of Jesus Christ, or even a book that speaks of Jesus but denies His position as Savior and the Son of God, can easily lead one astray.

God has promised us that we will have a reliable recording of His Word on which to base our paths and our decisions. In Psalm 18:30, the Bible tells us, "As for God, his way is perfect: the word of the LORD is tried: he is a buckler to all those that trust in him."

The Holy Bible is the only guideline to which I will unhesitatingly trust my eternal life.

3. I have a capable Guide. *In John 14:16, Jesus Himself promised us, "And I will pray the Father, and he shall give you another Comforter, that he may abide with you for ever."*

The Comforter to whom Jesus referred is none other than the Holy Spirit, the Third Person of God Himself, a wonderful, perfect, and wise Guide who chose to dwell within me when I accepted salvation through Jesus Christ.

In John 16:13, Jesus Himself tells us "when he, the Spirit of truth, is come, he will guide you into all truth: for he shall not speak of himself; but whatsoever he shall hear, that shall he speak."

This passage shows us that the Holy Spirit is a direct conduit to and a personal connection with God the Father.

My cave-diving instructor knew intimately every crook and cranny of the caves in which I trained. At every junction, he knew what would lie on either side. Oftentimes, it was only his knowledge that would save me from being frustrated or lost—given a choice between a broad, wide passage and a narrow, tight tunnel, I would probably be tempted to take what looked like the eas-

ier way—but my instructor would know that, in this case, the more difficult route was the only one that led to daylight.

In following him I knew that I could have confidence; I would be safe if I stayed under his guidance.

God not only knows the world we live in; He created it. He also knows and has always known long before they ever happened, every trial, every temptation, every difficulty, weakness, doubt, or fear we have encountered or will encounter in our lives. God the Father also knows and is willing to convey through the Holy Spirit the way out of each one of those difficulties. I must confess that I have often been resistant to His advice—it seemed more sensible to me to take what looked like an easier way. But always, I would learn that what seemed easy at the outset became difficult later on; I needed to learn to have the faith to trust the Holy Spirit and obey His counsel.

So—what about you? You're in the cave right now—we all are. The question is, do you know where you are going, or are you lost *within that cave?*

Several times now, when I've visited the Florida springs, I have met individuals who obviously were neither trained nor ready for the challenges and peril of the cave environment, yet they tried to shrug off the danger: "I won't get lost. . . . It can't happen to me. . . . I'm not going into the dangerous part. . . . Don't worry— I'll be fine."

That sort of stubbornness and arrogance is like spinning the chamber of a revolver and then putting the gun to your head. Eventually, tragedy will strike.

It's the same thing with our lives. Every day we go through without Jesus is another spin of the revolver cylinder, another unguided trip into the cave.

In 2 Corinthians 4:3, the Bible says, "But if our gospel be hid, it is hid to them that are lost."

A lot of the divers who refuse to get proper cave training are victims of their own pride. They don't want to admit that they

56

weren't born with the ability to navigate a difficult, peril-filled environment; what they don't realize is that no one is.

Cave divers are made that way, not born that way. It's the same thing with all human beings; we are born into a sin-stained world, and if we want to be cleansed of sin, that cleansing will have to be provided to us through the unworldly intervention of Jesus Christ. As Jesus Himself puts it in Matthew 18:11, "For the Son of man is come to save that which was lost."

So let me ask the question again: What about you? Time is getting shorter. The number of breaths you have remaining is getting fewer. Are you headed toward the light, or are you lost within the darkness?

Look at what it says in John 8:12: "Then spake Jesus again unto them, saying, I am the light of the world: he that followeth me shall not walk in darkness, but shall have the light of life."

It's true. Jesus is the one sure Guide, the only way to heaven.

Don't get me wrong. Even if you're ready, even if you have accepted Christ as your Savior, you will probably still have moments where you are frightened, nervous, uncertain of where to go, or even filled with great dread.

The difference is that, without Jesus, those moments are mounting elements of a greater tragedy. But with Him, they are simply transient difficulties, memorable chapters in a great and glorious adventure: one that leads, wonderfully and magnificently, up through unmarked passages and onward—to the Light.

THE
ALGONQUIN BEAR

*I will meet them as a bear that is bereaved
of her whelps, and will rend the caul of their heart,
and there will I devour them like a lion:
the wild beast shall tear them.*

HOSEA 13:8

It was a fine summer morning at the university. Birds
trilled from every tree, the thermometer lingered well
below the sweltering numbers, and the shade was still on
the streets. A perfect morning for a run.

I took the stairs two at a time in the recreation building. There was more than the balmy weather to my good
mood.

Three months earlier, dreading the prospect of spending a summer cooped indoors, teaching remedial compo-
sition to a group of students who'd rather be doing just

59

about anything else, I had proposed a new course—one on daybooks and diaries. Visiting the head of my English department with more zeal than foresight, I had proposed that we have students read the classic diaries of Samuel Pepys, Henry David Thoreau, and the like and then ask them to keep their own journals, to discover the form from the inside out.

And—here was the clincher, as far as I was concerned—in order to give each student equal fodder for his or her writing, we would take them all on a wilderness trip and ask them to write as we traveled.

My planned collaborator in this endeavor was Ed Rhudy, an old friend and climbing companion and a professor in the university's Recreation and Leisure Education department. I had chatted with Ed about the possibility of team-teaching a course in the summer, assuming that he would be taking a group into the mountains.

For the students, such an approach had the merit of offering credit for two courses for little more effort than they would have expended in taking one. Ed would be primarily responsible for the wilderness aspects of the course; I would be primarily responsible for the literature-and-composition content, but we would each share our knowledge in one another's area. As Ed usually suggested that the students keep journals on his trips, anyhow, the workload would not significantly increase, but the experience would be enriched. It sounded perfect.

When my department head approved the idea, though, I discovered that the Recreation department's summer trip would not be out west as I had assumed but up north to Algonquin Provincial Park in central Ontario. The students would be backpacking, which was no problem at all for me, but they would also be canoeing.

And canoeing was a problem.

It wasn't that I didn't know how. I'd spent summers in the Boundary Waters area near Eli, Minnesota, and I was adept with a paddle in lakes and rivers alike. But there was a hitch.

I couldn't swim.

When I'd finally admitted this to Ed, three weeks after we'd begun the classroom work for the course, he'd been both alarmed and astounded. Swimming is a basic skill for anyone planning to travel in a craft as capsize-prone as a canoe. And teaching canoeing without having that skill? That, as Ed calmly told me, was unthinkable. So he blocked out a weekend and quietly, patiently, and privately taught me—not only how to stay afloat and swim but the basics of lifesaving, as well.

The following week, when we took the class into the pool to practice emptying and regaining capsized canoes, no one but Ed was the wiser as to the recency of my watermanship.

Now, with that impediment behind us and a week to go before our departure for Canada, things were looking uniformly positive. Ed and I were healthy as horses, in the peak of condition, physically ready to handle anything the trip could throw at us. The students were healthy and fit, their boots broken in, their personalities compatible. We'd purchased all of the provisions but the fresh food, the long-term forecast looked acceptable, and half the class had gone beyond my basic reading list to discover the works of Robert Service and Norman Maclean. But when I stopped into Ed's office to roust him for our morning run, he looked concerned.

"What's up?" I asked.

He handed me the morning's paper, open to an inside page.

The story, datelined Algonquin Provincial Park, reported that two fishermen had been killed and partially consumed by a black bear over the weekend.

I looked up from the paper, stunned.

Black bears are omnivores that rarely exceed three hundred pounds in weight. While they occasionally attack humans, it is almost always in defense of a cub or an attempt to get at a food cache. A man-eating black bear is almost unheard-of; that is generally the province of the larger brown bears, the grizzlies, and the Kodiaks, which grow to be three to seven times larger than their black-coated cousins and are not native to southern Ontario.

The usual problem with black bears is that they are intelligent enough to become pests, overturning garbage cans, breaking into vehicles, and raiding tents for food.

A few years later during a climbing trip in western Wyoming, I would stay up half the night with a tree limb and a pile of rocks, batting pebbles at a male black bear that seemed doggedly determined to investigate my tent.

A ranger had warned me of this particular animal on the hike in. He was a "last year's cub," a juvenile that had stayed with his mother even after she had given birth to her new litter. As such, by the time the sow drove him off, the young animal was fully mature but had not yet developed the skill of finding, on his own, the berries, grubs, and fish that constitute 90 percent of a wild black bear's diet.

He had discovered, however—presumably through handouts—that hikers were a handy food source. Once he grew large enough to daunt hand-feeders, he had turned to theft for his livelihood, and he had already destroyed two packs and a tent in his forays around the lakeshore where I would be camping en route to my climb.

Eventually, after forty-five minutes of vigorous billy-pan banging and threatening shouts, I would connect with a blistering line drive, swatting a thimble-size bit of granite that stung Junior on the extremely sensitive tip of his leathery black snout. He would turn and bolt into the darkness, bawling pitifully for the mother that had long since abandoned him.

That sort of thing was what I pictured when I thought of troublesome black bears. This was entirely different. I could not have been more surprised had Ed handed me a clipping about a man-eating Labrador retriever.

Since the attack had gone unwitnessed, it was impossible to know exactly what had transpired. Both fishermen had been killed, so it was possible that a pair of bachelor males, possibly littermates, had been the perpetrators. Then again, another feasible scenario was that a single bear had first attacked one fisherman and then turned on the other when he rushed to the assistance of his friend.

Either way, it was serious news. One always accepts a certain element of risk when venturing into the wild; it is part of the environment. But to lead a group of novices into an area where a known lethal threat awaited—that was another thing entirely. Ed had been in contact with the park, which reported that trackers were attempting to locate the rogue animal and that, in the meantime, most of the wilderness permit holders scheduled into the park over the next fortnight had already canceled their trips.

Our class would not be meeting again for a couple of days. Ed and I decided to wait and see what transpired.

The next day brought an update: A suspect animal had been located and killed. Human remains had been discovered in its digestive system.

Both pieces of news had already circulated among the students by the time the class next met. Ed and I postponed the tent-pitching activity, gathering the class for a short meeting.

Black bears, we explained, were part of the Algonquin environment, had always been and, hopefully, would always be. When we ventured into the park, it would be our group that was intruding upon the bears' domain and not vice versa. We would have to show certain measures of respect in bear country, keeping temptation out of the bears' reach by hanging our food in "bear bags" several feet above the ground, cleaning our cooking utensils promptly, and scrupulously barring snack food from the tents.

Still, we added, exposing oneself to a higher-than-normal risk of attack had not been part of the prospect when the group had signed up for the course. Although a bear had been killed, we could not be certain that it was the sole animal responsible for the attacks. Nor could we discount the possibility that whatever circumstance had prompted one bear to kill—be it illness, a lack of normal foods, or some unknown condition that had caused it to be more defensive than usual—would not move another to do the same. In the end, conscience required us to put it to a vote; if anyone had second thoughts about going, we would cancel the trip and attempt to find a replacement destination or simply drop the course if that proved unfeasible.

We distributed slips of paper, asking the students to mark an "X" if they wished to go, an "O" if they felt we should cancel.

When we collected the ballots and turned them up on the desk, there wasn't an "O" in the lot. Relieved, Ed and I thanked the group for their attention and led them out to the lawn to practice pitching the tents.

We drove two vans up to Ontario, five people in each, both cargo areas packed to the headliners with food, backpacks, and duffle bags. The drive was the same as any such drive, the students joking a little too much in the discomfort of embarking on an unfamiliar experience, the miles getting wearisome near the end of the day. We reached the park after dark, setting up in a public campground near the headquarters building. The area was mostly deserted, an odd sight in high summer, and the few neighbors we had were all sleeping in trailers and recreation vehicles; ours was the only group in tents.

The next morning, when we drove over to the canoe livery, a ranger was waiting. He filled us in on the recent attacks, the killing of the suspect animal, and the further information that the bear population in the park was at an all-time high, making extraordinary precautions necessary.

"Will any of you," he asked, "be carrying writing materials with you into the backcountry?"

We all laughed and raised our hands. The ranger broke into that uncomfortable sort of smile a person displays when he hasn't gotten a joke.

"Great . . ." he said uncertainly. "We'd like you to record where you see bears and when, along with whatever details you can get from a safe distance—the approximate size of the animal, whether it's a lone animal or a sow with cubs, any unusual behaviors—that sort of thing."

That we would be seeing bears passed as sort of a given. We made a date to meet the ranger back at the livery in one week's time, loaded our canoes, and pushed off, the waters of the lake glass-still, a gently lifting fog setting just the right quality of mystery for a voyage into the unknown.

We decided to keep the first day's journey short. Although everyone in the class had been hiking to toughen their feet and leg muscles, they had not been canoeing, and we didn't want to overdo it. We made camp on Caroline Island, a minute, granite portion of the Canadian Shield, lifting its head just above the cold waters of the lake. A stand of pines provided just enough of a fir-needle blanket for us to pitch our tents, and the open water on both sides promised spectacular views of both the sunrise and the sunset. As we sat to make our journal entries after dinner, we were entertained by a distant laughter, the maniacal cries of loons.

The island camp also lessened the group's bear concerns. Black bears do swim—can swim quite well, as a matter of fact—but the chances of a bear crossing more than a quarter-mile of water to approach an inhabited island seemed slim. We relaxed and enjoyed our first evening of camp life.

I had acquired a 35-mm camera, a black-bodied Pentax, two years before, doing well enough in an undergraduate photojournalism course to be offered a part-time position as a laboratory assistant. I had brought the camera along on this trip, hoping to shoot photographs to accompany my journal and perhaps to get something good enough to publish—I had already taken a few steps in that direction.

I remember some of the photos I shot that first evening—Ed peering into the mouth of a steaming billy-pot, the sun hanging low over a peninsula heavy with fir trees, one of the students strumming a small guitar (a luxury we would carry on the canoeing leg but relegate to the van when we went backpacking).

And I remember thinking that evening that the black bear had become the icon of the trip. I had brought a small zoom lens with me—not a true wildlife-photographer's telephoto, but something that would do in a pinch—and I was looking forward to recording *Eurarctos americanus* on film.

The prospects for photographing bears appeared excellent. Since leaving the canoe livery's docks, we had not seen a single living soul beyond the ten modern-day voyageurs in our party. We had completed the first of our four scheduled portages just after noon that first day, leaving the only lake in which outboard motors were permitted and further assuring that we would travel in relative isolation (as it happened, we would not meet another human being until the final day of that week, when we paddled out).

In a park with its bear population at an historic peak, we were seemingly certain of sighting a black bear. Yet it did not happen that first day, nor did it happen the next.

On our third day into the backcountry, we rounded a peninsula in the early morning and came upon a section of marsh. Through the mists rising from the water, we saw a shape emerging, formidable in size and mysteriously vague.

A bear? We all stopped paddling and let our canoes drift, half out of curiosity and half out of dread. As we got closer, the shape materialized, a hulking creature with a horse-like snout, surmounted by a gigantic pair of antlers.

It was a moose, a big male, feasting on the tender roots of aquatic plants. He chewed tranquilly as we drifted past, then turned and waded back into the mist. It was such a perfect entrance and exit that one of the students wondered aloud whether the park kept a spotter and a pen of moose, releasing one whenever a flotilla of canoes drew near.

We spotted three more moose, another male and two females, in the days that followed but did not catch so much as a glimpse of a bear. Peregrine falcons, eagles, and the occasional deer showed up as we glassed the shoreline during our journey. Raccoons appeared regularly to test their ingenuity on our bear bags, and a porcupine lumbered through our camp one evening, stopping to sniff at the fire-ring before ambling on. We even heard the calls of wolves one moonlit night. Their ursine cousins were, however, nowhere to be seen.

This came as a matter of some relief to most of the members of our group, but it vexed me. As we paddled out, I scrutinized the water's edge, trying to peer more deeply into the shadows beneath trees, hoping to catch a glimpse of an ambling shape. I was also training for a climb that summer, so I did every portage at least twice, carrying canoes by myself and trying to trot silently, my camera bouncing on its neck strap, at the ready, should I turn up a bear on the trail.

Finally, when we'd made our last portage and had begun to see other craft, fishermen, on the water, I conceded to myself that there would be no bears on this leg of the trip.

I was deeply disappointed. After all the talk about black bears over the past two weeks, I had begun to take it as a certainty that we would see some and that I would able to photograph them at my leisure, with sufficient time and opportunity to compose not only an acceptable but an extraordinary image. Having invested seven days in the backcountry, I'd expected some fruit for our efforts. To see none was perplexing.

If it was perplexing to me, it was absolutely baffling to the ranger who'd come down to the canoe livery to meet our group, clipboard in hand, hoping to get fresh data for his risk-assessment.

After the briefest of greetings, he asked, "So, tell me, where did you see the most bears?"

"We didn't see any," Ed told him as we tied secured canoes to the docks with short painters.

"Not any?" The ranger repeated it almost weakly. Then, as if he'd asked the wrong thing, he added, "Not for the entire week?"

"Not for the entire week," I agreed.

The ranger tapped his clipboard with his pencil.

"Are you sure?"

"We saw some moose," one of the students offered.

"Four of them," another agreed.

The ranger's bewilderment turned to slack-jawed astonishment.

"Four moose!" he gasped. "I've been working here nine years. I see bears every day on my drive in to the office. I've never—ever—seen a moose."

"We have pictures," I added, holding up my camera.

The ranger thanked us for our time and made his way back to his sage-green, government-issue sedan.

We stayed in the public campground again that evening, treating the students to a pizza and soft drinks. Very early the next morning, we struck camp and drove in the dark to the trailhead.

Compared to the loads one might expect on a climbing expedition or a military campaign, our packs were relatively light that morning—no more than thirty to forty pounds apiece. Even so, we would make a point of starting down the trail dressed a little too lightly for the weather; that would prevent overheating as we warmed up from the exertion of walking under a load. As the next week would wear on, our students would adjust to this, wearing sweaters or jackets right up to the moment we began hiking, then taking them off and stowing them away just before swinging the backpacks onto their shoulders.

This first day, though, they were uncomfortable. Dressed in light shirts and hiking gear, they were standing around, waiting for one another, and getting chilled in the process. By the time Ed and I locked the vans and hid the keys on the frame rails, the group was stamping to stay warm, apprehensive in the pre-dawn gloom.

They were all fit, and we made good time down the trail, but we were a noisy group of nomads. Some of the students talked to vent their unease over hiking into what could be a predator-populated wilderness. Others had laced "bear bells"—small, round, nickel-plated bells, the type one sees at Christmas—onto their boots, so they jingled as they walked down the trail. And none of the students had developed the veteran's habit of leaving ample distance between each hiker. They clumped together into a train, each person restricted mostly to a view of his predecessor's backpack, a jingling, chattering, heavy-footed parade that announced its presence long before it came into view.

Even with all the noise, we still saw some wildlife. Ground squirrels, confident in their ability to vanish into the trailside brush, stood on their hind legs to watch us pass. Jays chattered from the thick pines that grew on either side, their blue-gray plumage a counterpoint to the overwhelming green. Small reptiles clung to ferns, eyeballs swiveling like turrets to observe our passage.

Crossing a small stream, we captured a small frog of a species not familiar to any of us. As part of their kit, each student carried an identification guide: one would have a book on plants, another a book on birds, and so forth. So we carried the frog to our next rest stop, dug out the requisite guide to amphibians, and identified it. Then, as a group, we carefully took the tiny animal to a small lake and released it.

The water erupted as largemouth bass, several of them, rolled at the surface, striking hungrily at the newly arrived food. The frog surfaced twice, valiantly, and then was pulled under, a widening ring of water the only indication that he had ever been there. The unexpected display left several of our group visibly stunned; rather than returning our specimen to safety, we had inadvertently sentenced it to death. It was a microcosmic lesson, a minute display of the kill-and-be-killed way that life is lived in the wilderness.

Smaller animals may have tolerated our company, but the larger fauna—deer, foxes, wolverines, and, especially, bear—were conspicuous in their absence. My camera was always at the ready, hanging from my neck or looped onto my packframe, but all I shot were candids of my companions and frame after frame of empty scenery. The bears continued to elude us.

When wary, many larger mammals will turn nocturnal, foraging for food at night and sleeping in heavy cover during the day. As we camped near water every evening, I made it my habit to rise early before the sun was up and go quietly to the water's edge, in hopes that I might see a bear coming down to drink before retiring for the day. Had I actually seen one, it's doubtful that I could have gotten a proper exposure in such low light, but gallery-quality photography was no longer a concern. I just wanted to get a picture.

What I wanted didn't matter. Raccoons and other small animals came to drink, but the bears had apparently gone to bed by moonlight.

Midweek, we stayed at the same campsite for two days, letting the students rest and relax.

We were on the shores of the most amazingly clear lake that I had ever seen; from the rocky shore, one could see down to a pebble bottom, thirty feet below. A taste of this water left the hint of a lemonade-like flavor, and this was the explanation for the clarity. The lake had turned acidic from pollutants, the invisible, sulphurous discharges from coal-fired power plants hundreds of miles away, and the effects of this "acid rain" had upset the water's normal acid/alkaline balance. It had turned acidic, to the point that it could no longer support most forms of life, including the microscopic algae that cloud most freshwater lakes.

The acid-rain problem has since been brought under control by using low-sulphur coal and by installing smoke-stack "scrubbers" on generating plants, but that lake, deep in the Algonquin wilderness, was a startling picture of how human industry hundreds of miles distant can affect the wild world. The water was safe to bathe in and safe to drink. But we saw no life in it other than leeches, which we were careful to avoid. And the clear water was beautiful, in that sterile and barren manner in which deserts can have beauty.

We had class around the fire-ring both days that we were camped at the lake, but other than that, everyone was free to relax as they saw fit. Some of the students day-hiked to another lake to fish. Others sketched and wrote at the water's edge.

I walked into the forest and stationed myself in the brush, downwind from game trails, sitting motionless for hours and hoping for a bear. I got nothing for my efforts but a couple of ticks, which had to be painfully coaxed from my skin by holding a smoldering ember next to their blood-gorged abdomens.

On our second evening at the lake, I spoke to Ed. The cacophony of our group was sure to scare off any bears that might be foraging along the trail, and that was not all bad, but I wanted to travel silently to see if I could get close enough to a bear for a picture. I told Ed I was going to leave camp the next morning a half-hour or so before the group; I would hike to the next campsite, cache my pack, and walk back to meet the group and help anyone who was having difficulty in the latter section of the day's hike. This would allow me to cover some sections of the trail two, or even three times, increasing the likelihood that I would spot a bear.

Ed and I were up long before the students the next day, so we could strike our tent and I could carry it and my share of the kitchen kit during my solo hike. I left camp before the sun was up, the chattering of squirrels and jays greeting the gray in the eastern sky.

Long before he'd trusted me to carry a rifle, my father had taken me hunting with him, and he'd taught me to walk as a hunter walks, starting each step on the outside of the heel, and rolling to the ball of the foot. When done well, this is a virtually silent method of travel, even when encumbered by a pack, and I made my way smoothly down the trail, avoiding sticks and dry leaves and bending my knees slightly to cushion my footfalls even further.

Previously, I had traveled as part of a noisy group. Now I was alone, and the difference was immediately apparent in the sounds of the woods around me. More birds called from the pine branches, and I saw more small animals scampering over the heavy matting of pine needles on the forest floor. Occasional gnawing noises preceded the odd sightings of porcupines chewing at plant roots. When the trail followed a small river, I watched a muskrat as it swam down the stream, completely unaware of my observation.

I refined my stealth as I walked, emptying my water bottle so the liquid would not slosh within it and tucking my camera strap beneath my pack straps to keep the camera from jostling. When I neared clearings, I slowed and approached them at a barely perceptible stroll; in one open spot I stood and watched a red fox hunting mice for several minutes before she looked up, saw me, and walked off into the woods, glancing back frequently, as if wondering what manner of tree it was that wore a backpack and a felt hat.

I was getting close to the next campsite, no more than a mile to go, when I heard it, the sound of something moving heavily along the trail ahead. The trees were thick on that section of my route, and the path itself twisted, finding a way past gnarled roots and around the mounded, smooth humps of half-buried boulders. Standing in this serpentine pathway, I could not see what it was that made the noise, but I could definitely hear it, shouldering aside the underbrush and getting closer.

A bear? Silently, I advanced the film in my camera, getting ready for a shot.

The noise grew louder. I stopped walking and listened. What I had first taken for the sound of a medium-size animal, fairly close by, was now a large animal, still some distance away, but getting nearer every moment. Rocks rolled along the trail. Branches snapped with rifle-like reports. Something big was coming, and it apparently didn't care who knew it.

Suddenly, I felt very vulnerable. Small saplings growing among the larger pines at the trail's edge would make an exit difficult, should I have to bolt from the trail with a pack on. I started unbuckling my waist-strap. Even as I did so, I noticed how narrow the trail had become.

If a large bear met me head-on, the trail might be too tight for the animal to turn around, causing it to feel cornered and threatened. An attack now seemed virtually imminent, and my breath came heavy in my throat as I considered my predicament. I had no weapon of any kind but a small Swiss Army pocketknife. The camera suddenly seemed foolish, the backpack an awkward encumbrance that would delay me in my flight.

The noise came closer. Whatever was approaching was no more than thirty feet ahead; I could hear heavy, panting, breathing and I could just barely see small treetops swaying up the trail. Treetops swaying! The animal approaching was not just big. It was huge, much larger than three hundred pounds. I had a sudden, awful mental image of the most gargantuan black bear that had ever walked the earth, a monster easily capable of flaying two adult fishermen alive.

I tried to shed my pack, but my shoulder strap and the camera strap had tangled. The pack was now half on me, half off, dangling and half-strangling me, and making me even more awkward than I had been moments before. My confidence, my calmness, my resolve to get my picture, all vanished like a vapor. There was no one around to make me feel self-conscious, no need to display the proverbial stiff upper lip, so I felt free to relinquish myself to the grip of abject, absolute fear.

I scrabbled to free myself just as the approaching behemoth rounded the turn in front of me. It blotted out the sky, and I gasped.

It was a young cow moose, six feet tall at the shoulders and gangly with her adolescent awkwardness. She came around the bend in the trail at full trot and stopped dead when she saw me, her back hooves skidding into her front in a cloud of dust, a scant eight feet from where I stood.

For one long second she looked at me, quaking, her eyes white with fright, and then she turned and bolted up the hill next to the trail, trampling saplings flat in her haste to get away. Just as she crested the hill, I remembered the camera and raised it, getting a blurred, shaky shot of her tall, retreating hindquarters.

Trembling, I slumped against a tree and let my heart return to a more normal cadence. Minutes passed before I put the pack back on.

Years later, during a winter driving trip through Alaska's Denali National Park, I would encounter more moose, two large bulls, which actually charged my car. I backed away from them in reverse gear until I reached a wider spot on the snow-covered road, where I tapped the brakes, spun around, and continued my retreat at full throttle.

Afterwards, I would learn that I had been lucky. A bull moose in full rut is nothing to toy with. They'd been known to charge locomotives head-on; an automobile's thin sheet metal would have done little to slow one down.

Several things had worked in my favor during my trail encounter in the Algonquin woods.

First, it was summer, too early for the rut. Second, my moose had been female, literally easily cowed. And third, she was young, unused to hikers, and still afraid of people, a quality that many large animals lose in places frequented by human beings.

Had she been male, or an older animal with a calf, I might not have escaped unscathed. Had she been a large bear, armed with sharp claws and canines, I very probably would have been at peril for my life.

The photographs for which I'd been hoping seemed suddenly far too costly.

Wiping my brow, I adjusted my packstraps and started up the trail to the next campsite.

Stealth was no longer important. I put the lens cover on my camera, and whistled as I walked.

"Be sober, be vigilant;" 1 Peter 5:8 admonishes us, "because your adversary the devil, as a roaring lion, walketh about, seeking whom he may devour."

There is a pulpit-worn admonition that "sin will take you farther than you wanted to go and keep you there longer than you wanted to stay." The reason we hear it so often is because it's true.

The same thing can be said about temptation. In fact, in His Sermon on the Mount, Jesus drew no distinction between entering into temptation—contemplating a wrongful deed—and doing the deed itself (see Matthew 5:28).

Temptation can lead us to danger. It can lead us to sin, and it can lead us to ruin.

Years after my heart-stopping encounter on the trails of Algonquin Provincial Park, I would read with newly appreciative eyes the words of Psalm 95:8, "Harden not your heart, as in the provocation, and as in the day of temptation in the wilderness."

Heart-hardening—stubbornness—comes all too easily to most of us. It can get us into situations for which we are not yet ready, and it can take us places where we should never venture at all.

As my friend Ed so rightly pointed out to me, there is absolutely nothing wrong with going canoeing in the Canadian North Country. But there is everything wrong with even thinking of going canoeing—anywhere, anytime—if you can't stay afloat, should you fall in.

By the same token, there are actions and activities that can please God if we do them in the way that He has ordained but that displease Him if we ignore His will.

God wants us, for instance, to love. Love is the divine emotion; it literally comes from God. And God will bless a loving relationship between a man and a woman, and will bless the intimacy between the two of them—provided they have first been bound together in the ordinance of a godly marriage.

Yet, if those same two people seek intimacy without marriage—if they even contemplate it, or toy with it, no matter how firm their resolve not to go past a certain point—they will offend God and injure themselves.

Some people won't agree with this. Some people will say, "It's nobody's business but our own, and what we're doing doesn't concern anyone but ourselves." But, according to God's Word, that's simply not true. It does concern Someone else. It hurts Someone else. It hurts the loving God who made us.

In Ephesians 4:30, we read, "And grieve not the holy Spirit of God." From that, we understand that we should turn away from sin and that, when we do sin, it not only hurts God, it moves Him to grief.

The most insidious thing about temptation is that it comes in degrees. I have a good pastor friend who often says, "There is a line between right and wrong, and wise people not only will not cross the line—they won't go anywhere near it."

When I broached my idea about a wilderness class with my university department head, there was nothing wrong with it; in fact, one could say that it was a laudable display of initiative. When Ed and I decided to go to Algonquin Provincial Park, again there was nothing wrong; thousands of people go there every year—it was established so people could enjoy the wholesome activities of canoeing, hiking, camping, and fishing in God's unspoiled wilderness.

When our group voted to continue with our plans, despite the fact that a bear attack had taken place, it was still a defensible action—the suspect bear had almost certainly been destroyed, *and we had a plan in place to lessen any remaining possibility of danger.*

But when getting a photograph of a bear became such an obsession that I began to place less value on my own safety, I was getting close to the line. When I decided to hike alone to get my picture, I was on the line. And when I deliberately walked in a stealthy fashion, so as to get closer to a bear than it might otherwise allow me to get, I crossed the line and placed myself in mortal danger.

Had someone asked me a few weeks earlier if I would be willing to walk silently down a trail where a large, rogue, man-eating animal might be waiting at any turn, I most certainly would have refused to entertain the thought. But temptation drew me nearer, step-by-step, like a rube following a dollar-bill attached to a thread, until finally I willingly put myself in precisely that situation. That I am here to tell the tale today is due solely to the fact that God chose to send a cowardly moose, rather than a raging bear, down the trail to meet me.

Temptation is anything—or anyone—that might lead you to a place where the Holy Spirit does not want you to be. It can come in a bottle, a can, a capsule, or a cigarette paper. It can be the person who urges you, step-by-step, closer to an activity or a place you know you should avoid. It can be the door, the book cover, or the computer screen that opens to a place where a holy God refuses to dwell.

Wherever we encounter temptation, the Bible is clear on how we are to deal with it.

God's Word tells us, first, to avoid temptation. In Proverbs 4:14–15, God advises us, "Enter not into the path of the wicked, and go not in the way of evil men. Avoid it, pass not by it, turn from it, and pass away."

We all know how to pick up on the warning signs that we're headed the wrong direction. We've all heard people tell us to stay away from certain places, certain people, "You don't want to hang around with them—they're bad news." When we ignore those warnings, we're walking straight toward the line that divides the safe from the unsafe.

Since there is a strong, ancient, and shrewd adversary who would like nothing better than to lead us across that line, we need the help of Someone who is even stronger to help us resist. We need to pray.

Jesus knew that and taught that. On two occasions, once in the Sermon on the Mount (Matthew 6:9–13) and once when one of his disciples requested instruction after Jesus had finished a time at devotions (Luke 11:2–4), Jesus presented almost exactly the same model prayer, and both times it contained the words, "and lead us not into temptation."

In the garden at Gethsemane, His sole admonition to His disciples was (Luke 22:40b), "Pray that ye enter not into temptation."

Clearly, our heavenly Father wants us to seek His help when temptation beckons.

He wants that, because He knows there is no temptation we cannot overcome with His help. In 1 Corinthians 10:13, He promises us that there has "no temptation taken you but such as is common to man: but God is faithful, who will not suffer you to be tempted above that ye are able; but will with the temptation also make a way to escape, that ye may be able to bear it."

Oftentimes, the key to escaping temptation can be found in Scripture. Remember, Jesus Himself was "led up of the Spirit into the wilderness to be tempted of the devil," (Matthew 4:1). When that happened, Jesus rebuked the devil with God's Word, knowing that there is no situation Satan can invent that has not already been anticipated—and countered—by God the Father.

Rest assured that temptation will come. You can avoid it in its most obvious forms, but, in its other incarnations, it follows us, even when we are closed into our own rooms, seemingly shut away from the world. It follows us in our thoughts and waits there, beckoning us nearer. But its presence does not mean that it will prevail. God provides us with a way out, and when we take it and give Him the victory, we please Him. The very first Book written in the New Testament, the Epistle of James, tells us this:

"Blessed is the man that endureth temptation: for when he is tried, he shall receive the crown of life, which the Lord hath promised to them that love him" (James 1:12).

Bears still walk the earth in Algonquin Provincial Park, as well they should, since that is where God put them. And I still own a camera—several, in fact. But for some years now I have not felt even the slightest urge to go back and roll the dice with my life in the hopes of getting a picture.

That is a temptation that has passed. Others will come, but, with God's help, I know that I can see victory over them, as well.

4

METAMORPHOSIS

*And though they . . . be hid from my sight
in the bottom of the sea, thence I will command
the serpent, and he shall bite them.*

AMOS 9:3

The southern stingray can inflict one of the nastiest wounds in the sea—a pencil-size puncture that penetrates deeply into the flesh and that often will not heal without prolonged medical treatment.

So when, on my first morning's dive with a charter boat out of Parguera, Puerto Rico, I deliberately approached a stingray resting on a deep sand flat, it came as no surprise that the divemaster immediately began rapping on her scuba tank with her dive knife, trying to warn me away.

I signaled back that I was fine and that I was aware of the stingray's potential to harm. Then I asked the divemaster to watch as, controlling my breathing to minimize the bubbles from my scuba regulator, I slowly approached the ray and began to softly stroke the edge of her sand-dusted disk.

The stingray fluttered slightly, as if debating flight. Then she gingerly raised the edge of her disk nearest me, exposing the velvet-soft, white underside. Responding to the invitation, I stroked there as well, and the ray immediately calmed.

Behind her scuba mask, the divemaster's eyes were wide with wonder. To all appearances I was petting a potentially dangerous animal. But from the ray's point of view, I was doing something quite different.

By "petting" the stingray, I was mimicking a common seafloor behavior. Underwater, resting animals are often approached by small fish and shrimp, which rid the larger animal of parasites by cleaning and devouring them from its skin, mouth, and gills. By stroking the stingray, I had convinced it that my hand was such a fish; when it raised its disk, it displayed a willingness to be cleaned. Implicit in the bargain was the understanding that it would not sting or behave aggressively while it was being cleaned.

Within five minutes, the divemaster had joined me on the sand flat, and I was showing her how to mimic the cleaning behavior herself. From her initial alarm, she had progressed to "petting" stingrays as well.

That moment with the stingray was no isolated incident. I have held moray eels, octopuses, and even small sharks in my arms. In Palau, I remember swimming slowly toward the surface through a liquid, living school of hundreds of barracuda, the predators forming a living circle around me so I could pass through their midst.

And years of underwater photography have blessed me with a high degree of "fish sense," as well. I have learned how to swim parallel with an animal and slowly close on it that way, rather than swimming directly toward it. When predators are about, I have placed myself near exit points, so prey fish will swim past me. I have acquired tricks for hovering motionless, even in relatively high current. I have learned, in short, to appear benign—which, for a great many years I was, going time and time again into the undersea environment and never harming a single living thing.

Then *Sport Diver* magazine asked me to do a piece on underwater hunting—spearfishing—and the prospect gave me pause.

It was not that I'd never hunted. My father hunted the fields and prairies of my native Illinois, and he brought me to the sport at such an early age that I cannot recall any time when I did not know how to load and fire a rifle or a small-gauge shotgun. Pheasant, quail, squirrel, and other small game often graced the table in my boyhood; I'd grown up viewing rifles and shotguns as tools for the gathering of food, in that respect, little different from bushel baskets or hoes.

Nor was it that I did not eat fish. Whenever I am near the sea, little else finds my table. And I'd often photographed friends spearfishing, so I knew it to be one of the most selective ways in which to harvest seafood—more discerning than hook-and-line and far more discriminating than the drift nets and dragnets used in the commercial fishing industry.

In short, although I'd never spearfished, I could not, in all conscience, do anything but approve of the practice. Besides, I've never had much patience with those people who condemn hunting even as they slice into a sirloin or wear Italian-leather loafers—as if such things fell placidly from the cattle-tree. There's a certain reality that must be owned up to, and I've always thought it must be better for a creature to die swiftly and cleanly in the field than terrified in a crowded slaughterhouse. So I've never viewed hunting as cruel.

But to carry a speargun into an environment where I had never done anything more than observe and interact? It seemed almost a betrayal of sorts.

Soul-searching led me to two options: I could turn vegetarian, or I could accept the assignment and go spearfishing.

In my mind, broccoli has always been, and will always be, a side dish. I called *Sport Diver* and told them I would go.

Later that summer, in mid-August, I was gearing up on the deck of the *Outrageous VI*, a charterboat out of Beaufort, North Carolina, getting ready to make a dive on a wreck called the *W. E. Hutton*—a freighter that had been torpedoed by German U-boats during World War Two.

As shipwrecks go, the *Hutton* is little to write home about. The Coast Guard depth-charged and then wire-dragged the wreck to keep it from becoming a hazard to navigation, and the result is a scattered, widespread debris field, full of twisted metal girders and explosion-warped steel plate. Close scrutiny is necessary even to gauge which end of the wreckage represents the stern and which was once the bow, and that most enjoyable aspect of shipwreck diving—going inside the wreck—is not possible on the *Hutton*, simply because there is no "inside" to it.

But for spearfishing, the *Hutton* is fertile ground. Migratory black grouper often hunt among its cover during the summer, and amberjack feed there on the bait fish that are attracted to any sort of sea-bottom structure.

That sharks might be there, as well, was pretty much accepted as a given. Our charter that day was composed entirely of a handful of journalists, including one or two divewriters and Marty Snyderman, an underwater photographer and documentary filmmaker who had come to the Outer Banks because he specialized in sharks. The most common shark on Outer Banks wrecks was the sand tiger, a large and fierce-looking but relatively docile creature;

several other species also hunted there, however, and could put in an appearance on virtually any dive.

Marty was there to shoot photographs of sand tigers and, as the *Hutton* wasn't known for attracting this species, he and most of the other divers had decided to sit this one out. The only ones going in would be my photographer and myself.

Underwater, as on the land, every region has its own peculiarities when it comes to catching fish. Knowing this, I'd asked the boat's first mate to take a look at my spearfishing gear, and he'd pronounced my JBL Sawed-Off Magnum speargun, with its tethered bronze shaft and winged rock-point tip, to be perfect for Outer Banks waters. But when he looked at my stringer, he'd frowned.

"We'll get greater Atlantic barracuda congregating under the boat once we've anchored," he told me. "And they hunt almost entirely by sight. If they see fish on a stringer, they'll go after them, so it's better to put the catch in a bag."

He produced his own catch-bag, a two-foot-by-three-foot canvas bag equipped with a nylon mesh drain-seam and a wire-bail latching top. The bag had seen some wear; the wire bail was bent and had to be opened with two hands. But I had no bag of my own, and I knew that greater Atlantic barracuda could approach eight feet in length. I gladly accepted the mate's suggestion and clipped the catch-bag off on my buoyancy compensator.

My photographer and I entered the water and saw immediately that the visibility, which had stood at better than eighty feet on earlier dives that week, had dropped to only half that. Rainstorms that had moved through the afternoon before and the beach run-off carried out with the low tides had sullied the waters, making it impossible to see the bottom seventy feet below.

Not that it mattered that much to me. My speargun was equipped with a shock-cord-dampened tether that was only seventeen feet long, a feature that allowed one to handle a struggling fish, as well as a precaution against losing a shaft in bluewater—deepwater—hunting. That being the case, I was concerned mostly with near-range visibility, which was fine, and as for my photographer, she was using a wide-angle lens, which tends to make most water appear clearer.

But while slightly turbid, the water was warm, every bit of seventy-eight degrees on the Fahrenheit scale. The Outer Banks is legendary with fishermen of all kinds because the Gulf Stream, which runs sixty to seventy miles offshore during the winter, moves in close to North Carolina's barrier islands during the summer.

This is the same Gulf Stream that washes the islands of the Caribbean, and, because it brings warm Caribbean water north with it, the Stream makes summer dives off the Outer Banks look more like a trip to the tropics than a plunge off America's mid-Atlantic coast. Tropical fish follow the Stream north, feasting on the nutrients that thrive in warmer waters, and spearfishers off the Banks can bag a combination of North Atlantic and subtropical species on the same dive—a combination unique to those waters.

On this dive, the first game fish to pass near us on the way to the bottom was a school of amberjack. Remembering that these fish have to be fairly large to be legally speared, I cocked all three of the surgical-rubber tubing slings on my gun, took aim, and squeezed the trigger.

The gun's aluminum stock jumped as the spear-shaft leaped out, and the group of amberjack turned as one body as the spear seemed to bounce off my target.

Of course, it hadn't. Underwater, objects appear about 25 percent larger—and an equal amount closer—than they actually are, and while I knew this, I had neglected to take it into account for my shot. The fish had appeared to be about fourteen feet away, meaning it had actually been seventeen-and-a-half. My spear had stopped six inches short.

I made a mental note to restrict my shots to targets that seemed about a dozen feet away, or closer. As I slid the shaft back onto the speargun and slung the tether between the front of the gun and the trigger, my photographer and I continued to sink toward the bottom.

Halfway down, details began to emerge in the underwater mist. I could pick out sections of broken piping—one with a toadfish peering, hermitlike, out of the end—shattered fragments of hull plating, pieces of ventilator shaft, and twisted steel I-beams. And then, among the wreckage, I saw a dark shape slowly making its way—a black grouper that looked as if it could feed two people, easily.

Pointing so the photographer would know what I was after, I recocked the speargun, changed my angle of descent slightly, and came to a hovering stop three feet off the bottom and about twenty feet to the side of the fish. Then I began swimming parallel to it. Using the same skills I'd learned hunting fish with a camera, I slowly closed the gap, keeping the grouper on my right-hand side, never pointing my body directly at it, because a head-on approach is always viewed as aggressive in the underwater world.

Finally, after two careful minutes of stalking, I'd closed to within a dozen feet of the fish. Still swimming parallel to it, I raised the gun like a long pistol, slowly bringing it to bear on the grouper, cocking my head only a tiny bit, so I could catch it at the periphery of what I could see through the dive mask.

Then, when I was certain that I was at the right distance, I turned my head, taking aim as I did so, and squeezed the trigger.

The photographer's photostrobe flared as my spear leapt free of the bucking gun. There was no short shot this time, the spearhead passing cleanly through the medium-size fish at the upper juncture of the gill-plate. It was a perfect shot, one that would damage the heart as well as shocking the brain, and the fish flapped feebly only twice before going still on the sinking shaft.

I brought it to me by the tether, congratulating myself on what had to be beginner's luck. The spear tip had spring-loaded wings, much like the wings on the hardware one would use to hang a swag hook from a ceiling, and these had sprung free on impact, swinging out after the tip had passed through the fish and trapping it there on the end of the spear. This feature made it impossible to pull the fish free of the tip, but the spearhead was threaded on. By unscrewing it, I could slide the fish off, and this is what I did. Trapping the grouper under my arm, I used both hands to open the catch-bag and secured my prize.

With the bail securely shut, I threaded the head back onto the spear and reloaded the gun. The photographer and I had discussed several "set-up" shots before we left the boat, and we did those next, pantomiming our intentions to one another, with her photographing me from several angles as I drew a bead on an imaginary fish. One photo we particularly wanted was a three-quarters-angle shot of the speargun being fired, so, as my photographer composed shots with me to one side of the viewfinder image, I shot the speargun at nothing, letting her freeze the bronze shaft as it flew into the empty part of the picture.

We did this five or six times before she was certain we'd gotten the image we wanted, then I went back to hunting.

I got a hogfish next, a moderate-size fish that I did not shoot as cleanly as the first, my low hit leaving the fish crippled but not dead. It was then that I realized I'd brought nothing along with which to "priest" the fish—most spearfishermen carry fairly large dive knives, so they can brain crippled fish with the heavy pommels.

My only knife was a small, flat, skeleton-handled number, and hitting the fish with this seemed only to hurt it further. Feeling more than a little guilty, I put the hogfish into the catch-bag. Blood appears green in the water at depth, and as I reloaded the gun, the bag quivered as the hogfish flipped its tail, and a faint green fog drifted up into the water around me.

As we neared forty-five minutes in the water, another black grouper appeared, this one nearly twice as large as the one in my bag, and I immediately began to parallel it, trying to close the gap to firing distance. But this fish had not achieved his size by being stupid. He had obviously been shot at before; twenty feet was as close as he would allow me to get before he would turn and scurry to another part of the wreck. Trailing him, I knew I was getting farther and farther from our anchor line, but this did not concern me, as both my photographer and I were well accustomed to making reference-free ascents. A few minutes later, my dive computer's face blinked as it winked into decompression mode, telling me that I would have to stop at ten feet for five minutes before going to the surface. But again, this did not bother me; I was trained in decompression diving and did it often in my shipwreck- and cave diving.

A couple of minutes later, I had lost the grouper in a particularly dense tangle of wreckage. My photographer drifted around to the front of me, raised her camera for a shot, and then pulled it away from her face, eyes wide. Like an inept pantomime of a salute, she whisked her right hand to her forehead, her fingers stiff and vertical.

Divers' hand signals vary in different regions of the world, but this one is the same wherever you go. It means "shark," or, done very rapidly, as my photographer had done it, "*shark!*"

I whirled around to see a sleek gray body, perhaps eight feet long, glide past in the near distance. It disappeared into the gray-blue mist, then reappeared a few seconds later, its snout wagging slowly from side to side like a tracking hound sniffing at the air.

There are a few circumstances that call for ending a dive immediately, and a big, inquisitive shark is one of them.

Turning back to my photographer, I jerked my thumb upwards, and the two of us began immediately to ascend.

As we closed on thirty feet, I checked my dive computer and saw that my decompression obligation had grown to ten minutes at ten feet. This would diminish a bit, I knew, the higher we got in the water column, but it would not go away entirely. I swam to my photographer, checked her computer, and saw that she was clear. Having stayed above me as she took most of the pictures, she had not absorbed as much nitrogen and could go straight to the surface in perfect safety.

Then a movement caught my eye in the middle distance. I looked up to see the shark orbiting us about forty feet out, its body winking into and out of definition as the visibility opened and closed around it.

I remembered a time, a few years before, when some of the people I was diving with had told me about a particularly troublesome shark that had troubled so many spearfishers that it had to be destroyed. Sharks are notoriously hard to kill because the shark's blood-filled liver occupies nearly two thirds of its abdominal cavity, and it pumps most of its blood by the simple action of swimming. Even a shark shot through the heart can live for hours before it finally bleeds out.

That particular shark had been killed with a powerhead, a special spear carrying a tip armed with a large-caliber handgun round. On hitting the shark, the round had been driven back against a firing pin, firing the bullet, even though the bullet had been incidental to what happened next. The explosive shock of the burning powder and the trauma of the compression wave it generated throughout the shark's body were what did it in.

A shark has no bones in its body, only cartilage, infinitely more tough and elastic than bone and far less prone to fracture. When that shark had finally been winched aboard their vessel, my friends had debated whether a speargun could penetrate it, and finally, one of their group, a big, burly fellow who'd played linebacker in college, had raised a heavy hunting knife and brought it down with all the force he could muster on the shark's head, directly above the brain. The blade had penetrated perhaps a quarter of an inch before coming to a quivering stop. And that had been a smaller shark, only about six feet long.

That being the case, I entertained no illusions about my abilities to dispatch an eight-footer with a speargun equipped for shooting panfish. I was fairly confident, though, that I could keep the shark at bay by using the uncocked speargun as a prod. But the first thing to do was to get my unarmed photographer to safety. I pointed at her, then gave her a thumbs-up, pointed at my eyes, and finally cupped my two hands in front of me: *You go up to the surface and look for the boat.*

She nodded and began to ascend. As she did so, I allowed myself to drop about ten feet deeper, and noted that the shark adjusted its depth to stay even with me as it circled. The hogfish flopped once more within the canvas catch-bag, and another thin mist of brownish-green blood wafted out into the water around me.

Sharks can detect infinitesimal amounts of blood diluted in seawater, although I doubt it was the blood that first drew my visitor. More likely, it was the repeated heavy thrumming sound as I fired the speargun for the camera. Sharks are like cats—curious—and it was probably curiosity that drew this shark in.

She circled—I could see that it was a "she" by the fact that she had cloverleaf-like fins around her anal vent, rather than the claspers of a male. This gave me no consolation; female sharks grow larger than their male counterparts and, because they have to hunt more often to sustain a larger physiology, they tend to be proportionally more aggressive. I turned in the water to keep her in sight, and she circled closer—close enough for me to identify her as a sandbar shark, a thick, wedge-headed species that is known for being far more aggressive than common reef sharks.

When she closed to within twenty feet, I scissors-kicked myself forcefully in her direction, at the same time jabbing the speargun toward her. I got no closer than ten feet, but this piking action, which is viewed by all animals in the sea as a posture of attack, did the trick. The shark spooked away, fleeing into the mist like a scared cat.

Within a minute she was back, though, circling again. And, as I turned to watch her, I detected more movement at the edge of my vision. It was another shark, about the same size—my predator had been joined by a sister.

Above me, I heard the hollow metal rap of a dive knife against a scuba tank. I looked up, past a group of four amberjack that swam between us, making the surface appear impossibly far away, and saw my photographer pointing, indicating the direction of the boat. I noted the bearing with my compass, at the same time checking my decompression computer: five minutes left before I could ascend.

Pointing to my photographer, I extended all five fingers of my hand in the direction she'd indicated: *You—swim to the boat.* She paused for a moment, hesitant to leave me alone, and then did as I suggested, wisely resubmerging so she would not splash at the surface and draw the sharks. I watched until she was out of sight, glancing from her to the circling sharks and back again. If one of the sandbar sharks broke away to pursue her, I had already resolved to shoot it and take my chances with whatever followed. As it turned out, though, both of the sickle-mouthed intruders decided to stick with me.

Later I would learn that, almost as soon as she'd reached the surface, my photographer had hailed the boat, calling out, "Tom's got sharks on him!"

At that, Marty Snyderman, easily the most knowledgeable person about sharks on the Outer Banks that day,
had jumped up, tossing his scuba tank and buoyancy compensator on over his head, settling it onto his shoulders
right over his T-shirt, and walked purposefully toward the
Outrageous VI's swim deck, scooping up his mask and fins
and buckling his BC into place as he went.

"How many?" Marty had called back, noting that the
photographer had said "sharks" and not "a shark."

My photographer had ducked back under for a quick
look, and at that moment, the four amberjacks had swum
back between us, looking, due to a trick in perspective,
much larger than they actually were. In her haste, my photographer counted everything as the same species.

"At least six," she had told Marty . . . and he had stopped
buckling his gear.

Marty knew that two divers could probably fend off one
or two moderate-size sharks. But if six sharks were swarm-
ing, introducing another diver into the mix could actually
exacerbate the situation. And it didn't make sense to place
two divers at such grave risk, rather than just one. Marty
had wisely stopped short of the swim deck and begun removing his gear.

Back underwater, it was, of course, only two sharks I
was dealing with. But I was getting little comfort from the
fact. The two big sandbar females may only have had
brains the size of walnuts, but they were using them, circling 180 degrees apart from one another, so I could keep
my eyes on only one at a time.

They were wary. The sound—or rather the heavy underwater vibrations—from the speargun may have first
attracted them, but they were now so close that the scent
of blood in the water had to have been nearly overwhelming to them. They were, after all, animals that

preyed upon others for their sustenance. Yet they could see that I was obviously uninjured.

Most free-ranging sharks also possess the ability to detect even weak electrical discharges in the water, and now they were, even as they circled, picking up the energy created by the pulse of two hearts. One was the heavy—and, by this time, no doubt wildly accelerated—product of a large mammalian heart. The other was the thready and feeble signal from the heart of a weak and dying fish. And while the former made them cautious and was keeping them temporarily at bay, the latter called them nearer and nearer, with a siren song irresistible to animals that had been killers since birth. They were wary, but they were getting closer.

The first shark was now less than fifteen feet away, the other a little farther out. Both were close enough that I could see detail—the little pilot fish fluttering like battle banners in the bow waves over their broad heads; the outer of their seven rows of sharp, white, triangular teeth; the five gills rippling in the dappled light from the surface twenty feet above.

Again, I piked with the speargun, first one way and then the other, and both times the sharks fled, but, both times, they returned within seconds. And each time they returned, the circles shrank by a foot or two.

Three minutes. The computer said that I could surface in three minutes. Indeed, the decompression had shrunk close enough that I felt I could probably dispense with the rest of it with relative safety, but swimming for the surface seemed ill-advised with two agitated sharks so very near at hand.

Two minutes. The nearer shark broke away from her circle and passed within a yard of me, her head moving side to side, the minute indentations of the sensing organs under her snout sizing me up, trying to gauge whether I was timid or a threat.

She turned and came back, this time bumping my leg with her thick torso, the sandpaper-like surface of her tough skin rubbing a frazzled spot in the nylon outer fabric of my wet suit. It was the kind of move a school-yard bully would make, shouldering aside a youngster to see if he would object.

And, because I did not respond with sting, or shock, or bite, or any of the myriad defenses of the sea, the shark now knew all that she needed to know. She banked in the water like a fighter plane and came straight at me.

Trying to keep the speartip between her and me, I scrabbled at the catch-bag, attempting to dump my catch. It was useless. The bag would not open one-handed.

The shark kept coming, her lower jaw open and pronated forward, her eyes rolled back to cover them for the attack.

A hundred wishes crossed my mind. I wished that I had waited for clearer water, so I would have seen the sharks sooner. I wished that I had not stayed down so long, forcing my dive into decompression. I wished that I had stayed nearer the anchor line. I wished that I had not chased that last grouper. I wished that I had brought another armed diver with me. I wished the boat were closer. I wished that I were out of the water. I wished that I had cocked the speargun.

That last thought, I knew, was nothing but the sheer edge of panic trying to force its way over my horizon. Shooting the shark now would do nothing but enrage it, put more blood in the water, and provoke its companion into outright frenzy.

But I remembered something I'd always heard, that a shark's nose is extremely sensitive. Somebody—a surfer I'd spoken with in California, I think—had told me that, if all else fails, punching a shark in the nose could . . . might . . . break off an attack.

I clenched my fist and then thought better of it. I needed that hand for writing, for fly-fishing, for holding in the throttle on the airplane during takeoff, for all sorts of things. Thrusting it in the vicinity of a few hundred razor-sharp, slashing teeth just didn't seem like a sound idea.

But I did have the speargun. And even though I wasn't about to shoot the shark, the gun did have a broad, hard, molded-nylon butt. As the shark closed in, I kicked hard with my fins, moving aside like a matador performing a Veronica with a charging bull. As I did so, I turned the gun around in my hands, raised it, and then brought it down squarely on the shark's nose with all the force that I could muster.

From wrists to elbows, my arms reverberated as if I had struck an inch-thick steel hull plating with a sledgehammer. To my great surprise, the speargun remained unbent and in one piece.

As for the shark, she closed her mouth on nothing, moved slightly aside like a pedestrian making her way down a crowded street, and kept swimming past me, her great, vertical caudal fin not even missing a beat. Gracefully, she turned in the water and then slowed, looking at me with an expression that seemed to say: "So? Is that it? Is that all you've got?"

It was not. I still had the fish. And even though I could not open the damaged bail with one hand, it only took two fingers for me to operate the brass clip that secured it to my buoyancy compensator. I unclipped the bag, held it out, waving it with a "here-kitty" motion, and then using large, deliberate and obvious gestures, I dropped it.

Still slowly moving toward me, the shark turned toward the falling bag, turned back toward me, and then searched after the bag with her snout. Satisfied that the small, bleeding fish with the feeble heartbeat was in the white canvas object that was drifting downward, she moved her caudal fin once and shot downward in pursuit.

My entire body shuddered with a sigh of relief. I looked at my dive computer and saw that it had gone clear. Then, suddenly, I froze.

The other shark. Where was it?

As if in reply, a tremendous pressure wave of moving water shoved me down a good foot, as a great, gray-white body arched over my shoulder like a dolphin jumping its trainer in a show. The left pectoral fin actually brushed my hair, pushing it forward, and then all I could see was the undulating caudal fin as the hungry sandbar shark drove down after her companion.

Thirty feet below me, the canvas bag spun slowly downward. After it, the two sharks followed in sharp spirals, twisting like warplanes in a dogfight. They had not yet caught the bag when the underwater mists swallowed them, and then they were gone, as if the drama of the previous ten minutes had been nothing but a dream.

I swam to the boat, where I did not have to climb the ladder to the *Outrageous VI's* swim deck. Four sets of arms reached down and plucked me whole from the water, speargun, weight belt, scuba tank, and all. Eight eyes searched me anxiously, looking for blood. Eight ears waited for what I had to say.

I turned to the mate.

"I'm sorry," I told him. "We need to stop in the dive shop together when we get back to port—I owe you a new bag."

In Matthew 28:19, Jesus Himself commanded his disciples, "Go . . . and teach all nations." In Mark 16:15, moments before

His ascension into heaven, He delivered a similar command, telling His followers to go "into all the world, and preach the gospel to every creature."

"All nations. . . ."

"Every creature. . . ."

As many commentators have pointed out, this injunction is remembered not as the Great Suggestion but as the Great Commission; there was nothing arbitrary about Jesus' parting words to His followers. It is not the choice but the duty of every Christian to share his or her faith with others and to give others the good news about how they, too, can find salvation from sin's consequence through Jesus Christ.

Nor did Jesus restrict, in any way, the scope or the territory in which His disciples were to do their work. Every person, no matter who they are or what society might think of them, is to hear the news of what Jesus Christ has done for them . . . because, in hearing, they may believe, and in believing, they become children of God, every bit as precious to Him as you or me.

During His earthly ministry, Jesus literally lived His own admonition. Three of the four Gospels (Matthew 9:10, Mark 2:15, and Luke 5:30) record the fact that He would sit down to meals with "publicans" (hated bureaucrats who abused the power of the law to extort money from the common people) "and sinners" (the word used in the original language of the New Testament denotes not simply someone who has sinned but a person seemingly committed to a life of sin).

Jesus was roundly and forcefully condemned by the religious establishment of His day for this conduct. They considered Him guilty by association, calling Him (Luke 7:34) "a gluttonous man, and a winebibber" (a drunkard, or wino).

But Jesus persisted in the practice, freely associating with the dregs of society—willingly putting Himself into awkward or even dangerous situations that most people would do just about anything to avoid. The first time He declared that He was the Messiah promised in Scripture, He did so (John 4:26) to a woman who was a Samaritan, a member of an ethnically mixed group considered untouchable by devout Palestinian Jews. And when He went to raise Lazarus from the dead, He traveled into Judea, a region in which people lived so contrary to His teachings that they had sought to stone Him to death (John 11:7–8).

Bible readers sometimes wonder what to think of Jesus' actions in light of such Scripture passages as Titus 2:14 and 1 Peter 2:9, which call for Christians to be "a peculiar people," and 2 Corinthians 6:17–18, in which God says, concerning worldliness, "come out from among them, and be . . . separate . . . and touch not the unclean thing; and I will receive you, and will be a Father unto you."

If anything, James 4:4 puts a similar admonition into even stronger terms, saying, "a friend of the world is the enemy of God."

Citing verses such as these, many Christians over the centuries have virtually (and sometimes literally) cloistered themselves away from worldly influences. They have developed what they believe to be a sense of propriety and an aversion to anything that does not fall into their definition of what is appropriate and correct.

Introduce a drunkard still reeking of his Saturday-night celebrations into a company of Sunday-morning churchgoers, and the chances are that most of them will avoid even eye contact with what they consider to be an undesirable intruder. Bring a prostitute or a known and convicted criminal into the Lord's house on a Sunday morning, and some church authorities might go so far as to order their eviction.

Yet the Bible tells us that Jesus took the gospel to drunkards. He often associated with and addressed women of low repute. And the last human being He addressed before dying was a convicted thief (Matthew 27:38) to whom He promised an eternal reward in heaven (Luke 23:43).

In the years that I've been diving, I've often been in the water with sharks, sometimes with sharks so numerous that I've found them impossible to count. I have photographed unpredictable mako sharks while the guides on the dive boat above me ladled

raw chum into the water and, on the day following my con-
frontation with the two aggressive sandbar sharks, I was diving
less than an arm's length away from a full-grown sand tiger
shark, in the narrow confines of a shipwreck.

On one dive off Long Island in the Bahamas—a dive on a coral
outcrop where white-tip reef sharks were regularly fed—I vividly
remembered being inspected at extremely close quarters by the
predators as they tried to determine which of the divers in our
group was carrying the bucket of frozen fish for their feeding.
During a dive in the shark channel at the Curaçao Seaquarium,
the curator threw mackerel into the water around me to attract
sharks within camera range, while an assistant hovered nearby
to fend off overly inquisitive sharks with a "shark billy"—a short,
lightweight length of PVC pipe.

But on all of those dives, I have never felt anything near the
level of the threat that I felt on that spearfishing dive off the Outer
Banks.

What made the difference? It was this: On all my previous
dives, I had been in the ocean environment, but I had not been
a part of it. I was among the creatures of the sea. But I was not
the same as them.

On many of those earlier dives, I had made efforts to blend in
with my surroundings. In Great Exuma, for instance, Ed Haxby
had taught me to hover motionless, so the fish would view me as
part of the reef. And in Micronesia, local divemasters had shown
me how to anchor myself into dead coral with a short length of
cable and then add air to my buoyancy compensator, so I could
hang motionless in the current, a horizontal form a few feet off
the reef—a trick that convinced the local black-tip sharks to accept me as one of their own.

But there is a world of difference between camouflage and com-
pliance. When I took and then carried wounded fish in the undersea world, I became a predator in a world of predators. Predator fish, like the carnivores of the land, will often steal prey from
one another and will even attack one another and battle over
wounded, weakened prey. This is the natural order of the ocean.

100

So the danger I felt myself in on this particular dive was not the result of anything having changed in the sea. It was the result of the fact that I had changed from an observer of the food chain to a part of it. Had I not killed and then carried fish—the natural food of sharks—I doubt deeply that either of the big predators would have shown anything more than a passing interest in me. I found myself in danger, not because I had entered the sharks' world, but because I had crossed the line and become a part of that world.

During His ministry in Palestine, Jesus sat down to meals with, and even stayed in the homes of, publicans—people who extorted money from others (Matthew, who became an apostle and wrote the first Book of the New Testament, was a publican when he first met Jesus). Yet Jesus never took from anyone; He only gave.

And, while the Bible records many instances of Jesus being present where people were drinking and very probably inebriated, it goes without saying that Jesus, who inspired Ephesians 5:18 ("And be not drunk with wine, wherein is excess; but be filled with the Spirit"), was never intoxicated.

Though He preached to people who were guilty of fornication, Jesus remained chaste. When He entered the temple and spoke with the prideful Pharisees (the religious leaders of his day), He was humble. In the midst of angry crowds, He could be an island of calm, whose manner affected all those around Him (John 8:7–9).

In fact, although Jesus suffered crucifixion to pay for the sins of all mankind, He never sinned. Exodus 23:33 makes it clear that the very essence of sin is an offense against God, and, even while incarnate in human form, Jesus, as the Son of God, was literally incapable of committing an offense against Himself.

Other verses of Scripture confirm this. Hebrews 4:15 says Jesus "was in all points tempted like as we are, yet without sin." In 1 Peter 2:22, we learn that Jesus "did no sin, neither was guile found in his mouth." And 1 John 3:5 plainly says of Jesus that "in him is no sin."

Jesus, in short, was fully capable of going out into the sin-filled places of the world without becoming part of them. And He saw going into such places as a necessity. When the Pharisees questioned this, Jesus explained (Mark 2:17): "They that are whole have no need of the physician, but they that are sick: I came not to call the righteous, but sinners to repentance."

Skittishness over even the semblance of worldly influence is nothing new in the Christian world. Even in today's most traditional churches, for instance, the songs written by Fanny Jane Crosby (hymns such as "Blessed Assurance," which is familiar even to many non-churchgoers) are sung with gusto, yet they were broadly condemned in their day. They sounded like the popular music of the time and not at all like the sacred music to which people were accustomed.

And concerns over ungodly influence are certainly justified. Isaiah 14:12–15 recounts the story of Lucifer, once a member of the host of heaven, who attempted to usurp God Himself. Lucifer's coup was a failure before it started, but he does retain control over the world in which we live: John 12:31 describes him as "the prince of this world." And so he uses the elements of this world to try to ensnare us. Genesis 3:1–7 tells how this adversary— whom we have come to know as the devil—used lies and guile to convince mankind to sin.

That the devil is still successful in this respect is overwhelmingly evident. Romans 5:12 says plainly that we "all have sinned." After all, other than Jesus, how many of the billions who have walked this earth have done so without sinning? Romans 3:10 gives us the sobering answer: "not one."

Obviously, there is a force afoot in the world that is interested in seeing people led astray from the will of God, and that force's success rate is a devastating 100 percent: every one of us has sinned. Given that, and given the fact that this world is, by definition, the devil's own province, it is understandable that many Christians are leery of it.

Yet Jesus Christ has told us to go out into the world to spread His gospel, and Jesus would never tell us to do the impossible.

How can we go out among people who need God and at the same time avert the devil . . . despite his pervasive influence? To start with, we can take solace in the fact that, if a person has desires to turn away from former ways and has accepted Jesus Christ as his or her personal Savior, then that person is what 2 Corinthians 5:17 calls "a new creature" and the devil's odds become dramatically reversed.

You see, even though the devil has led each and every one of us into sin, a believer in salvation through Jesus Christ—a repentant Christian—is also 100 percent certain to be treated by God as if he or she had never sinned at all.

Not that believers never sin. They do, and they will. But they possess a power that goes far beyond what they knew in their lives before Christ. They have a divine Sponsor—the Son of God, who has already paid for their sins with His own sacrifice on the cross and who stands ready to be an empowering and faithful Friend.

In the New Testament, Matthew 17:14–21 and Mark 9:17–29 recount the same event—that of Jesus' encounter with a young man possessed by a demonic spirit. None of the disciples had been able to cast the spirit out, yet Jesus did so with just a few words. And when the disciples asked why this was, Jesus explained that it was simply a matter of belief.

At the time of that event, although Jesus had worked many miracles, His crucifixion and resurrection had yet to take place. So, when it comes to matters of belief, we have an advantage in this day and age; while the disciples of the time had only the promise that Jesus was the Messiah and the Son of God, we have the proof. We know that He did what only God can do, and our belief comes that much more easily.

We can put that belief to work to keep the adversary at bay. "Resist the devil," says James 4:7, "and he will flee from you."

The devil and his minions are anciently shrewd and uncommonly crafty. But they all share the same fatal flaw; none were smart enough to side with right and perfection. As Christians, on the other hand, we are, and the result of that difference is that we have access to tremendous power over the devil and his followers. In 1 Corinthians 6:3, the Bible says plainly that we shall judge them. And Luke 9:1 tells us that Jesus Himself gave the disciples "power and authority over all devils."

So, alone, we have no power over the evil afoot in the world; we are vulnerable and certain to succumb to it. But with Jesus Christ in our hearts and the Holy Spirit dwelling within us, we have both the ability and the strength to go out into the world and spread the good news of God's gift—eternal reward in heaven for those who believe in Christ's sacrifice.

When I approached that stingray in Puerto Rico, I was interacting with an animal that could do me grievous harm. But I could reach out to it with safety, because I had knowledge of the limits to which I could go without putting myself at risk.

With the sharks, I knew the limits as well, but I crossed them. I had violated two rules—having blood about me in the water in the presence of sharks, and putting myself into a situation in which I did not have the option of leaving immediately once the sharks became aggressive.

In the same fashion, when I leave the refuge of church and family and Christian friends, I can do so with safety if I listen to what 1 Kings 19:12 calls the "still small voice" of God.

It is God's will, after all, that I should carry the good news of redemption to a world of lost souls. But it is never His will that I should get carried away by that world as I am abroad in it.

5

TRYING
THE TRIUMPH

In your patience possess ye your souls.
LUKE 21:19

In that hollow and echoing silence unique to the hours before dawn, I entered the nearly empty garage, pulling the door shut softly behind me, taking care not to awaken my slumbering neighbors.

A flick of the wall switch brought up a single sixty-watt bulb. Even in the feeble glow, the motorcycle, standing on its center stand in the middle of the concrete floor, gleamed like a new creation. Chrome handlebars swept up from either side of the canister-like speedometer and tachometer. A single headlamp squatted beneath them, as if hunched to stay out of the wind. The fuel tank and fenders were painted a reddish gold that the manufacturer had called "Olympic Flame Orange," in honor of the Munich Olympics, held the year the old bike had been produced. The long double seat had been cleaned, every tuck and rib rubbed with a vinyl protectant. The right-side oil tank, mirrored by the tool kit on the left, wore a shining finish of black lacquer. Every chrome spoke gleamed, and the tires—although two decades old and cracked with age— had been dressed to their original deep, jet black. Beneath the tank, the heart of the machine, a side-by-side twin-cylinder, half-liter engine, sat mutely on the black frame rails.

The motorcycle was complete, except for the mufflers— "silencers" in Britain, where the machine had been produced—and the foot-peg rubbers. These had aged beyond usefulness, the mufflers rusted where condensation from some short start-up years before had eaten them away from within and the sun-worn rubber of the foot-pegs crumbly to the touch.

But other than that, the motorcycle—a 500 cc, 1972 Triumph Daytona—had only one failing.

It would not start.

Actually, it was more than that. The pistons were frozen in their cylinder bores, the rings were locked into place by years of immobility, and residual gasoline had long since hardened into varnish.

At least, that was what I was gambling on.

My ownership of this particular motorcycle had commenced two weeks before, an unplanned—and entirely unbudgeted—event. A student at my karate dojo, one of my fellow black belts, had mentioned that he had an older motorcycle to get rid of. His wife had never approved of the noisy machine, which he had purchased new on a whim upon his discharge from the army. Now, he told me, he was finishing his course of study to become a pharmacist, and he needed five hundred dollars for books. It seemed only logical to reclaim a few feet of garage space at the same time.

I'd listened with middling interest until he mentioned that the machine in question was a 1972 Triumph Daytona, a relatively rare motorcycle, and one of the later creations of Edward Turner, Triumph's legendary chief designer. Then my ears really perked up. I'd told him to look no further for a buyer.

It was hours later, at his house, when we discovered that the pistons of the old motorcycle, which had been parked nearly a decade earlier, would not budge in their bores. My friend had been ready to call off the deal, but I stuck by it. If the motorcycle had been running when it was put away, I figured I would be able to get it running again, and it would be a bargain at the price I was paying.

But if I could not, I had just acquired a rather expensive piece of metal sculpture.

The Triumph came home with me that evening, strapped down securely in the back of the van. I backed it down a two-by-twelve board to my driveway and put it away, the motorcycle's only journey in the last eight years having been from one garage to another, and that not under its own power.

The next morning, with the garage door up to admit daylight, I pulled the spark plugs from the engine and, working with a penlight and a dental mirror, looked at what I could see of the cylinder walls. Only one piston was down far enough for a decent inspection, but the walls looked good, with the faint cross-hatching of the factory honing still showing and no scratches that might indicate a broken ring. A flake or two of light corrosion showed up as well. When a motorcycle is put into storage, the cylinder walls should be fogged by spraying storage oil into the carburetor throats until the engine stalls. Apparently, this had never been done.

I set the spark plugs aside. Putting a funnel into the plug holes, I filled the cylinders with Marvel Mystery Oil, a thin, top-cylinder lubricant packaged in an ornately printed, flat red can that might have been designed by Edward Turner himself. Then I replaced the spark plugs, screwing them in loosely by hand, and set about other tasks: draining and removing the gas tank and disassembling the carburetors, soaking the parts in a bowl of solvent.

After a couple of hours, I folded out the kick-starter, snicked the bike into neutral, and tried tapping the kick-start lever with a rubber-headed mallet. The lever didn't budge—I might as well have been rapping on the concrete floor of the garage.

Thus began a ritual. I was working in an advertising agency in those days and, every morning, before heading in to the office, I would go into the garage and give the kick-starter a tap with the mallet.

In the evenings, I worked on erasing the effects of the years on the old Triumph. The battery was useless, so I replaced it with one from a local discount store, no duplicate of the original being readily available. The rectifier was also hopelessly corroded, but I found an original-equipment spare at a British-only motorcycle hobbyist's shop about an hour away, where I also lucked onto an unclaimed special-order set of mufflers at a discount price.

Sloshing solvent around in the fuel tank cleaned it of the varnish left by vintage gasoline, and the oil tank got the same treatment. The screen that served as an oil filter was cleaned and replaced, and the oil impeller was rinsed and replaced in like-new condition. The carburetors, which were of the oil-dampened variety unique to old British cars and motorcycles, were rebuilt with new fiberboard gaskets, the brittle oil and gas lines were replaced with new ones, and the air and fuel filters were all discarded in favor of original-equipment spares.

The surface rust on the handlebars disappeared under an assault with chrome cleaner and elbow grease. And the paint on the fuel tank and fenders proved to be little more than dusty—washed and waxed, it gleamed as it must have the day that it was shipped from the factory.

Still, I wondered as I did all this work whether the labor would be for naught. I believed what my friend had said about the motorcycle having been in running condition, but if, for some reason, he was mistaken and the engine had seized, the cure was going to be expensive. At the least, it would mean new pistons, rings, bearings, and cylinder sleeves. At the worst, it could mean a new engine, and a non-original engine would halve the collector's value of the motorcycle.

For the moment, though, all I could do was give the kick-starter its daily mallet-tap and hope.

Then came that Saturday morning when I couldn't sleep, concerns over a project at work having pushed away the dreams. The Triumph had been resting with the oil in its cylinders for a full two weeks. I got up, dressed, went into the garage, picked up the mallet, and gave the kick-starter its by-now-customary tap.

It moved.

Amazed, I pressed the kick-starter with the heel of my hand and it moved further.

Forgetting the advertising project that had awakened me, I shrugged on my coveralls, removed the spark plugs, siphoned the oil from the bores with a length of plastic tubing, and mopped up the remaining drops with a judiciously rolled shop rag.

That done, I listened as I worked the kick-starter through a complete cycle with my hand. In each cylinder, air sucked in and was expelled through the open spark-plug holes. The sound was eerie, like the gasp of a half-drowned human being, reviving after a long time under-water.

In a matter of minutes, I had the spark plugs snug in their sockets, the distributor wires attached. The fuel tank was already topped off with fresh high-octane fuel, and the key was in the ignition switch, on the right side of the headlamp.

I thought about this as I opened the garage door to let in some fresh night air. The Triumph's twin carburetors were freshly rebuilt, and they had been set as closely as possible to their original specifications. But, since each car-buretor fed a single piston, they also had to be balanced, and it was one of those quandaries of mechanical engi-neering that the carburetors could only be balanced if the engine was running, and the engine would only run well if the carburetors were balanced.

Still, it was tempting to give the bike a try, just to get an idea of how much work was left before I could get it run-ning. I opened the fuel petcocks and, with the key still switched off, cracked the throttle as I pushed the kick-starter through half a dozen slow cycles, getting oil worked into and around the bearings and pulling fuel down into the float bowls. Then I switched the key on, stood tall on the bare metal of the foot-pegs, and let my weight drop on the kick-starter.

Instantly, the motorcycle roared to life, the sound of the unmuffled exhaust a shattering vintage thunder—like a .50-caliber machine gun being fired from a low-flying B-17. Yellow flame and smoke shot from the shortened ex-haust pipes just behind my ankles, and I twisted the hand-grip throttle back, bringing the engine to full crescendo, and watched in satisfaction as the yellow flames dimmed to soft blue, the residual oil having been burned away by the high-test gasoline.

Then lights began to wink on all around the predawn neighborhood, and I pressed the kill switch and shut the garage door, hiding the evidence of my predawn malfeasance.

The rest of that day was a pleasant blur of industry, as I mounted the chrome mufflers on the motorcycle and adjusted points and spark-plug gaps. Then, having waited until a reasonable hour, I restarted the now civilly muffled Triumph and worked on resetting and balancing the carburetors.

I had a pneumometric gauge to measure the amount of airflow passing into each carburetor, a device with a glass tube containing a colored plastic ball, but I soon settled into the old tried-and-true method of screwing one end of a length of plastic tubing into my ear and holding the other end to the throats of the running carburetors, adjusting the units until the hiss of the air rushing into the two throats was at the same pitch.

By noon, the engine was running smoothly both at idle and at full throttle, and an electronic tachometer jumpered into a spark-plug lead verified that the mechanical tach of the motorcycle was producing reasonably accurate readings. I pumped air into the old tires and took the Triumph for a careful turn around the circle on which I lived. Judicious application of the brakes produced an initial rasp as the shoes knocked corrosion off the drums, but this soon smoothed out, although the front brake cable had stretched so much that it barely operated. The speedometer was doing a passable imitation of Rip Van Winkle, resting at zero with the occasional spastic leap up into the higher numbers, but I decided to wait on this for a bit. It would either start working as lubricant got nudged into the dry spots on the mechanism, or it would have to be rebuilt, and only time would tell which of the two was true.

By 5:00, the motorcycle was as ready as I could make it. The new foot-peg covers—original-equipment replacements with the distinctive Triumph logo embossed into the rubber—had been tamped snugly into place. I also had a new set of folding pillion foot-pegs—for use by a rear passenger—but I was hesitant to put these on. I had taken a motorcycle safety course offered by a local club the previous weekend and had performed the emergency evasive maneuvers and mandatory operating skills well enough to re-earn a motorcycle endorsement on my driver's license, but I did not yet feel ready to take anyone else for a spin with me. In the end, I covered the rear foot-peg mount threads with brass acorn nuts, making it temporarily impossible to carry a passenger.

Dinner with friends kept me away from the garage until late that evening. When I got back, it was a beautifully dark June evening, with spring peepers calling in the distance and the first crickets of summer singing in some shadowy corner of the garden.

I looked in on the old Triumph. It was ready to ride . . . nearly. The tires still needed to be replaced, but I'd wanted to do that with Dunlops identical to the originals, and those had been a special order, not due at the shop until the following week.

I'd also yet to acquire the leather jacket that would eventually become a fixture on all of my rides, regardless of the temperature. Far from being a question of style, the motorcyclist's leather jacket is a safety accessory, providing a thick layer of abrasion resistance in the event of a fall.

And then there was the fact that it was pitch black that evening, with no moon and none expected. Legally, I was licensed to ride at night, but—with my only motorcycling in recent years having been parking-lot maneuvers during my safety course and the few laps I'd taken of our circle that afternoon—it really seemed prudent to do some daylight riding before I got on the road with only the Triumph's old twelve-volt headlamp for illumination.

I mulled all of this over and then decided that a denim jacket, while nearly not the same thing as leather, would provide me at least some measure of protection in a spill. As far as riding at night went, I figured that I would be safe if I stuck only to straight and predictable roads with low traffic. And I did, after all, have the helmet that I'd purchased for the motorcycle safety course only a week earlier.

Ten minutes later, the Triumph was roaring out of the driveway with me astride it. It had taken only a minute or two to find my denim jacket and an old pair of deer-skin gloves to protect my hands. The new full-face helmet fit snugly, and I rode with the clear plastic visor partially raised, letting in the cool air and the myriad fragrances of an early summer night.

The old motorcycle's headlight did even less to illuminate the road ahead than I'd expected, so I stopped at the end of our circle to adjust it, aiming it slightly downward. This did a better job of picking out the pavement just ahead of me, but it did nothing to bring objects in the near distance into better view. I switched to the high beam, which improved the situation only marginally.

I had a road in mind, a stretch of blacktop out in the country, about a mile north of my house. This was one of my regular bicycling routes, and I remembered it as being straight for virtually all of its length, with a smooth asphalt surface that had been replaced only that spring.

The shortest way there was a gravel road, a route that I was loath to try, given the possibility of scratching the Triumph's pristine paint. So I rode down to a state highway that ran a half-mile south of me and then took this east for another mile, where a paved county road would take me up to where I wanted to be.

There is a feeling to riding a motorcycle that is very similar to that of alpine skiing. Like a skier, a motorcyclist uses subtle shifts of weight and balance to control his course, and like skis, a motorcycle doesn't make a turn as much as it carves it.

I was rediscovering this sensation and reveling in it by the time I made the turn north. My helmet blocked the slipstream that would have made it a true "wind in the hair" experience, but I could feel my sleeves and trouser legs fluttering in the wind as I accelerated, and the denim jacket billowed away from my back as the machine thrummed on into the darkness. As I rode, I realized that I had left my boots at home and was riding in a well-worn pair of boat shoes, but to complete the ride would take only a few minutes longer than returning home, so I rode on, reminding myself that, even though the old white urethane bottoms of the boat shoes had all the adhesive qualities of a bar of soap, the foot-peg rubbers were brand-new.

The lightbulbs in the gauges had all been replaced as I'd gone over the motorcycle, so the white numerals showed quite clearly, despite the dark night, and the orange needle of the tachometer arced smoothly upward as I accelerated through the gears. The speedometer was still *hors de combat*, its needle jumping erratically like the confused blinking of a roused sleeper, so I had no way of accurately gauging my speed. But I kept the Triumph to what I assumed to be a safe pace, settled more comfortably on the broad vinyl saddle, and continued to enjoy the exhilarating feeling of my passage through the ebony night. While riding a motorcycle and riding a bicycle may appear to be one and the same skill, the fact is that the greater weight of a motorcycle dramatically lowers its center of gravity, relative to the rider, so a motorcycle at speed feels very stable and not the least bit prone to tip. I was rediscovering this, as well, and greatly enjoying it.

It was nearing midnight when I got to the asphalt road I'd been thinking about, and it was, as I'd expected, completely deserted, with not a headlight in sight in either direction. As I balanced the motorcycle with my toe-tips at the stop sign (for, although I stand six-foot-two and am rather long-legged, the Triumph is an exceedingly tall motorcycle), I could see that the fresh asphalt surface had lost none of its blackness, blending seamlessly into the moonless sky above. This being a slightly traveled county road, no white fog lines had been painted to mark the point where road ended and ditch began, but a thin course of white gravel at either side did a passable job of outlining the pavement, and the road ran, to the best of my recollection, straight east and west. It looked like as good a spot as any to give the classic Triumph a try. I turned east and rolled the throttle smoothly on.

All four gears passed in rapid succession, and I kept the throttle rolled back, feeling the old motorcycle gain speed and watching the tachometer needle creep up. The faster I went, the higher I revised my estimation of what constituted a "safe" speed. I consoled my conscience with the fact that, should my estimation of my speed conflict with that of the state's, the speedometer was, after all, inoperative, and I really had no idea how fast I was actually going.

I scooted back on the double seat and leaned forward so my chest was nearly touching the fuel tank, taking as much of my body out of the wind as possible and imagining what it must be like to do this in earnest at Laguna Seca or the Isle of Man.

I was hunched over the handlebars like this, and still accelerating, when a yellow sign bearing a serpentine arrow flashed by on my right, and, in the fluttering yellow circle that was the Triumph's headlamp beam, a gigantic, thick-trunked willow tree began to grow rapidly into resolution.

It was a powerful memory jogger, and it instantly came to me that this particular asphalt road did not run ruler-straight east and west for its full length, as I'd previously recalled, but jogged briefly south and then north again to

115

avoid a small pond and its accompanying stand of willows. The road was straight, except for that one obstacle.

This obstacle.

The willow gained detail at an alarmingly swift rate as the motorcycle and I hurtled toward it like a moth to obliterating flame. I remember the speedometer having one of its brief fits of wakefulness as this happened, and I recall how my dread deepened as the needle leaped abruptly through its full course of travel and bumped into the upper-range pin.

Not good.

Not good at all.

Braking was not an option with so brief a notice. The best that braking could do was slow my impact with the tree from one that would reduce me to an unrecognizable smear, to one that was merely fatal. It was either that, or, if I managed to avoid the tree, I would be catapulted out into the center of the pond, where the lily-dotted waters would forever hide the evidence of my folly. So I kept my left hand and foot off the brakes.

I had no alternative—I had to make the turn.

When driving a car, steering is fairly intuitive. One points the wheels in the direction one wishes to go, and the vehicle follows the path of least resistance. On a motorcycle, on the other hand, one steers by pushing the handlebar on the side to which one wishes to travel, in effect, turning the front wheel *away* from the direction of the turn.

This works because a motorcycle's tire is, like that of a bicycle, curved across the face of its tread, and "countersteering," as the technique is called, forces the tire to travel, not on the large circle of the center of the tire, but on a shallow cone of rubber between the center and the side.

If you lay a paper cup—one with a mouth wider than its base—on its side and roll it across a flat and level table, the cup will describe an arc toward its smaller side. A motorcycle tire can be thought of as two of these cups glued mouth-to-mouth. When balanced in the center, the cups will roll straight, but if tipped to either side, they will make a turn in that direction.

In my early days of riding motorcycles, I had learned this after a fashion, as I had in my bicycling (for bicycles turn and handle according to the same laws of physics as motorcycles), but my comprehension had only gone so far. I steered by leaning or, at low speeds, I pointed the front wheel where I wanted to go and shifted my weight to keep the motorcycle on its center line, making it turn like an automobile.

Much of the safety course I'd taken had been devoted to relentlessly drilling this tendency out of me, for the simple reason that a motorcyclist who jerks the handlebar into a turn in a panic is a motorcyclist destined to be separated from his steed. The instructors had begun by asking us to lean our motorcycles steeply to the left and cant the front wheels steeply to the right, then roll on the throttle from a complete stop. To everyone's amazement, this resulted, not in a group of motorcycles and riders lying on their sides, but in a uniform turn to the left, even at slow speeds.

We had proceeded, then, through cone-marked chicanes and white-limed obstacle courses, culminating in a drill in which we accelerated toward an instructor behind a barricade, who signaled at the last minute, by pointing, the direction in which we were supposed to turn.

Regretting that I never did so personally, I would now like to thank those instructors for their insistence, because it undoubtedly saved my life on that distant June evening.

The willow tree mushroomed before me, every detail of its ancient bark now starkly delineated in the brightening yellow circle of the headlight.

Rather than steering into the turn, as instinct demanded, I shoved the right side of the handlebar out and down, at the same time shifting my weight so that only my left thigh was over the saddle. From the hips up, I was in that position road racers refer to as "hanging out," my right knee pointed down and dangling only a scant inch above the rushing pavement.

No sooner had I done this than the road curved back to the left, forcing me to leap back over the motorcycle and hold on with my right thigh, this time countersteering forcefully against the left side of the handlebar. Then the road turned back to the east, and I swiftly shifted again, countersteering right, finally pulling back up to a neutral riding position as the road mercifully resumed its shot-straight course.

It was all over in far less time than it takes to describe it, the motorcycle and I describing a movement like two and a half swift beats of an old mechanical metronome: steeply tilting right, then left, then right again and finally, gradually rolling back upright as we caromed through the turn. That I made it through was due, not to talent or skill, but simply to the persistence of the training I'd received the week before, for I had not consciously thought about any of it. I had simply done it. There hadn't even been time to be gripped by fear; it had all flown past so quickly.

That came a minute or so later, as I thought of the fact that I had made three extremely aggressive turns in rapid succession on twenty-year-old tires—tires rotted to the point that they had no business on pavement—and had stayed on the motorcycle wearing shoes that should have, by any standard, slipped out from under me on the very first turn.

Sweating now, despite the coolness of the post-midnight air, I slowed the Triumph to a dramatically civilized pace and made my way carefully home.

The next morning, I carefully inspected the old motorcycle for signs of the previous evening's ordeal. At first I saw none. Then I looked more closely and noticed something curious about the foot-pegs.

Viewed from the end, they were supposed to be round. But both of mine looked more like the Greek letter *omega* (Ω), round on three sides, but flat on the bottom. Getting down on all fours showed me why: I had heeled the old motorcycle over so far on the turns that I had ground away parts of both foot-pegs—all the way through the tough urethane rubber and into the hard English steel beneath. Clearly, the pegs must have traced a bright shower of sparks through at least two of the three turns. Had I cornered just a fraction of a degree harder, I would have dug a foot-peg into the pavement to the point where it would have caught, sending the elderly bike into a spin. As it was, I had probably made it through upright simply because the asphalt was freshly laid, with no cracks on which to catch the grounded pegs.

Stomach aflutter, I hung up both my helmet and the Triumph's keys. My next ride would be in daylight . . . and it would wait until the fresh set of Dunlops had arrived.

"Patience," says the old adage, "is a virtue."
And so it is. In several places—Romans 5:3–4, 1 Timothy 6:11, 2 Timothy 3:10, Titus 2:2, and 2 Peter 1:6, to name a few—the Bible lists patience as one of the cardinal characteristics of the practicing Christian.

The church father, Augustine, is reported to have once written this short prayer: "Lord, grant me patience—but grant it now."

Amusing as this may be, it contains a grain of truth: Patience is a quality that runs contrary to human nature. If we desire it, we would be wise to seek it from the Almighty. Left to our own devices, it is too easy to be as I was with my old Triumph motorcycle—patient in some respects, but hasty in the ones that truly mattered.

I was, after all, able to resist the temptation to force the pistons in their cylinders, allowing the oil to do its work, trusting that the engine would free itself in its own time. Likewise, I put in the time and the effort to do the rebuilding, cleaning, and adjusting necessary to restore the carburetors, brakes, and oil system before starting the motorcycle—and I did this because to do otherwise would run the risk of damaging the valuable old Triumph.

But when it came time to exercise a bit of prudence, to wait just a few hours and avoid risking damage to myself, my resolve buckled. And this was a decision that, had it not been for the training I'd received, might have led to dire consequences.

Why did I take the Triumph out on that dark June night, despite my misgivings? I would say it was because I had convinced myself that the motorcycle and I were ready. And yet, if I had taken the time to search my heart and truly think the situation through, there is no way I would have come to that decision.

In Job 38:2, God rebuked Job for darkening "counsel by words without knowledge"—in other words, for confounding that which was right with that which merely sounded reasonable. I had done the same thing, making arguments that could not be borne out by fact. No amount of persuasion could make the Triumph's timeworn tires worthy of a trial on the pavement. And no amount of argument could contradict the fact that, having not ridden a motorcycle on the street for several years, I had no business reintroducing myself to the activity at night.

I should have waited. I wasn't ready. But I talked myself into it nonetheless.

120

God rewards patience . . . and God demands it. Look at David, who was anointed king of all Israel when he was still a boy (1 Samuel 16:6–12). Yet David honored Saul, the reigning king—even when Saul turned against him—and did not assume the throne until word came to him that Saul had perished in battle.

By this point, Saul had tried to kill David several times. He threw javelins at him. He led an army in search of him. A lesser man would have killed Saul himself, in preemptive self-defense, and no one would have thought the less of him for it. But when David was given the opportunity to do this, he did not. In 1 Samuel 24:4, the Bible tells the story of how Saul was out searching for David so he could kill him and had camped in a cave for the night. David crept into the cave and cut off a piece of the king's robe to show how he had been presented with the opportunity to kill his opponent but had spared him.

One result of this patience was that David became Israel's first great king, the father of Solomon, and the head of a genealogical house that, seven generations later, would culminate in the birth of Jesus Himself.

On the other side of the coin, we have, in the Book of Exodus, the story of Moses, who was born into a family of Israelite slaves but raised as an aristocrat in the royal house of Egypt.

While still a young man, Moses felt burdened for the afflictions of his people and killed an Egyptian who was brutalizing a Hebrew. A champion of the afflicted—who could fault Moses for being that?

God could—because God did not want a rebellion led by a man. God wanted a nation led by God, and to shed Moses of his impudence and teach him the humility and patience that he would need to be an instrument of the Almighty, God allowed Moses to go into exile and to serve as a shepherd until he was nearly eighty years old. Moses was elderly, even by the standards of his day, before God used him as His spokesman in Israel's exodus from Egypt.

So what sorts of patience does God expect from us? If we search His Word, we find that God asks us to be patient in three ways:

1. God asks us to wait patiently on His will. *"To every thing there is a season," says Ecclesiastes 3:1, "and a time to every purpose under the heaven."*

That time is, of course, the time of the One who created everything—God's time.

God has never missed a deadline, never arrived too late to accomplish what He wanted to accomplish, and never forgone an opportunity to work . . . even though, to our frail and flawed eyes, it may often seem that He has done every bit of the above. But the reason we think this is because we can only see what has happened, while God sees everything—present, past, and future—at once.

The eighth chapter of the Gospel of Luke tells how Jesus was summoned to the home of Jairus, the keeper of a Gadarene synagogue, to attend to the man's sick daughter. The eleventh chapter of John recounts Jesus' journey to the home of Lazarus, a good friend who had been ill on a previous visit. And, in both cases, the person Jesus went to see was dead by the time He arrived (in fact, in Lazarus's case, Jesus revealed to His disciples that His friend had died before He ever even set out on the journey).

To the people present in those two households, time had seemingly run out. A runner was dispatched from Jairus's house to tell Jesus not to bother coming, because it was too late and the girl had passed away. And when Jesus approached Lazarus's tomb, Martha (Lazarus's sister) objected, telling Him that her brother was not only dead and in the grave, but that the body had already begun to decompose.

Yet, in both instances, Jesus restored the dead person to life, just as he did the only son of the widow of Nain (Luke 7:11–15).

Time cannot run out on Jesus—time cannot run out on God—because God is not a slave to time. Time is a slave to God.

2. God asks us to be patient with others. *Our model for patience is God Himself. After all, He loves us and cares for us even before we come to accept Him. And because God demonstrates His patience to us, He expects us to do the same thing with those around us.*

"Have patience with me," says the servant in Matthew 18:26 as he asks his master to forgive him his debt. And the master does just that. Yet, in Matthew 18:29–30, that same servant refuses to have patience with his own debtor—an injustice for which he is ultimately punished by his master.

Patience was taught even by the hyper-religious Pharisees of Jesus' time, but theirs was a human sort of patience, with human limits.

Understanding, for instance, that man is inherently weak and prone to error, the rabbis of Jesus' day taught that one should forgive one's fellow man for his transgressions. But the religious Jews believed that a person had expressed sufficient patience when he forgave his neighbor three times for the same infraction.

In Matthew 18:21, Peter asked Jesus about this custom, but instead of three times, he substituted seven—in Hebrew numerology, the number of perfection. No doubt, Peter felt he was being more than generous. But Jesus replied that the proper number of absolutions was not seven, but "seventy times seven" (Matthew 18:22).

Seven is, of course, like three, an easy number to keep track of, but seventy times seven, or four hundred ninety, is an absurdly high number of indulgences to tally up. In fact, if one did, one would have to keep a record, and the very act of keeping such a record would imply that one was just waiting for his brother to fail—certainly not the sort of behavior that one would expect from a Christian.

Clearly, God expects us to have a bottomless well of patience when it comes to dealing with our fellow man.

All of us have people in our lives who try our patience. It could be a family member, a friend, a teacher, coworker, or a superior on the job. Sometimes, a friend's continual lateness for social events, or a child's ongoing disobedience, or a spouse's forgetfulness may even seem like some special torment designed for us and us alone. But it's worth remembering that, in the original language of the New Testament, "patience" and "endurance" are the same word. As Christians, we are expected to have the strength to carry on without allowing our tempers to flare.

How can we do this? As it is with so many things in life, "With men this is impossible; but with God all things are possible" (Matthew 19:26).

3. God expects us to be patient with ourselves. *All of us have expectations of who we want to be, what we want to have accomplished, and where we wish to have arrived by certain stages in our life. And virtually every human being will, at some point or another, reach that point, look back, and see goals that were not attained.*

Regret over such things is common, but it's not what God wants. He knows better.

"Like as a father pitieth his children, so the LORD *pitieth them that fear him," says Psalm 103:13–14. And the Psalm continues, "For he knoweth our frame; he remembereth that we are dust."*

Even Peter, the leader of the twelve apostles, and the man who was, with his brother Andrew, one of the first disciples called to follow Jesus, had moments when he expected more of himself than he could possibly deliver. In all four of the Gospels we have the story (Matthew 26:33–75, Mark 14:29–72, Luke 22:33–62, and John 13:37 and 18:15–27) of how Peter swore to Jesus that he would never abandon or betray Him—how he would stick with Him to the very death—and how Jesus told him not to expect so much of himself, revealing as He spoke that Peter would betray Him three times before an exact moment that very night.

That Peter later came to understand the principle of patience with himself is demonstrated by the fact that this incident appears in the Gospel of Mark—the one that was written down by Mark shortly after Peter's death, to perpetuate the account of Christ's ministry that had been preached by Peter himself. Certainly, Peter would never have told of this episode—which, by human standards, discredits him—if he had not understood the value of the lesson it conveys.

God presents every one of us with opportunities—doors through which we may pass and gain experience, knowledge, virtue . . .

and patience. Sometimes these doors are opportunities to minister. Sometimes they are new friends, new careers, or other new circumstances in life.

Sometimes they are old Triumph motorcycles.

One of the qualities that should distinguish us as Christians is the ability to wait until we can tell if those doors are open before we attempt to pass through. One way we can do this is through prayer. And if we pray to God for guidance, we can rest assured that He will answer. Guidance in our growth as Christians is, after all, one of the things God guarantees us in Matthew 21:22. There, He says, "And all things, whatsoever ye shall ask in prayer, believing, ye shall receive."

And you will.

6

THE JUMP TURN

Brethren, I count not myself to have apprehended: but this one thing I do, forgetting those things which are behind, and reaching forth unto those things which are before, I press toward the mark. . . .

PHILIPPIANS 3:13–14

Mid-Ohio Sports Car Course, that fabled racetrack in the countryside near Columbus, had just been freshly repaved. The July afternoon was warm but not hot, the kind of weather in which one could expect a good grip from the tires without worrying about them going slippery in the heat.

I headed for the first car in line: a jet-black Corvette equipped, according to the data sheet in my hand, with the Z51 performance package—the perfect car for a perfect track. Switching the open-faced helmet from my right hand to my left, I reached for the door and nearly bumped

127

into another fellow—also helmet in hand—headed for the same car.

Smiling to hide my disappointment, I stepped back, saying, "Go ahead."

"No, please," the other man told me. "You first. You're a writer, aren't you?"

I confirmed that I was—on long-lead assignment from a national magazine, writing about the new fall models.

"I'm with Chevrolet Engineering," my new friend told me as he nodded at the sports car. "I just wanted to see what this one could do. But you're working. You go first."

"Okay," I replied. "But why don't you ride along? I'll do three laps; then we'll pit and switch places, and you can do three. That way we'll both get to ride and drive."

"You've got a deal," he smiled, walking around to the passenger's side of the car.

My assignment had begun the day before, in Detroit, when Chevrolet Public Relations collected two or three dozen other writers and me at the conclusion of the annual Detroit Grand Prix. There were only magazine writers in our group; magazines require more lead-time to lay out and separate photography for their pages, and this would be the company's "long-lead" press preview. Although it was July, and we would each have our stories written and in to our respective editors by week's end, the issues we were writing for would not appear until mid-September, when the new models were due to arrive at dealerships. Newspaper writers and radio and television reporters—all of whom required only a day or two to prepare their material for release—would attend a separate "short-lead" media event, to be held later, in early September.

There is a tradition to these auto-company media events. The public-relations departments have long known that no amount of coddling will persuade the press to bring its praises to a less-than-acceptable product. Get them in the right frame of mind, though, and writers just might begin to see a good product as a great one, so the companies continually vied, trying to outdo one another in pampering the press.

The writers, of course, scoffed at this blatant apple-polishing. Still, in years of attending such things, I never once saw an auto writer refuse the PR department's efforts at hospitality.

For this press event, Chevrolet's PR people had chosen to open with a dinner cruise from Detroit, down the western shallows of Lake Erie, to a luxury hotel in Toledo, Ohio.

After a hot afternoon of watching the racing, my colleagues virtually swarmed into the vessel's big main dining salon, with some heading for the appetizer tables and the majority diverting to either of two long open bars.

As for myself, I stepped to the large, broad windows of the dining deck and looked at a wall of towering black clouds moving in from the southwest. The vessel had been chartered out of Ohio, and one could see in a glance that it drafted only a few feet of water, being designed primarily for river cruising. That, together with the weather moving in, promised an interesting ride. I sipped a bottle of mineral water and made myself a light dinner from the salad bar.

Our initial ride, down the Detroit River, past tree-green Grosse Isle, was uneventful except for the buildup of clouds to the west. As the captain announced that guests were welcome to visit the wheelhouse, my fellow journalists were attacking the groaning buffet with gusto. Then we reached the mouth of the river, and conditions deteriorated rapidly.

Lake Erie, despite being one of the smaller of the Great Lakes, is notorious for being one of the roughest in bad weather. The reasons for this are the lake's relatively shallow average depth, which amplifies wave activity, together with the fact that the lake runs west-to-east, in the same direction as the prevailing winds. This makes Erie very prone to seiching—a condition in which wind-driven water is pushed higher on one side of the lake than the other, until gravity finally returns it in a direction counter to the wind-generated waves.

Almost as soon as we entered the lake, the shallow-draft ship began to both pitch—bob up and down at the bow— and roll side to side in the waves. Within minutes, the heavily fed and slightly inebriated magazine writers were taking on a greenish cast, obviously feeling the effects of the waves. After half an hour, many were rushing out to the rail, oblivious to the gray sheets of rain that had begun to pour down.

All my life, I have had the extraordinarily good fortune of never once becoming seasick. Still, I did not want to tempt fate, and a roomful of retching, groaning journalists was not making for the best of company, so, remembering the captain's invitation, I made my way forward, past the busy heads (rest rooms) and up the stairlike ladder to the pilothouse.

On the bridge, the captain himself was at the helm, and the view was amazing, with rows of waves marching out of a dim gray horizon and crashing into our bow. The wheelhouse was glazed on three sides; the rain was smearing the glass except for two places, where spinning circular panes threw the water aside and afforded a relatively clear line of sight.

We were well off from the western shore, the captain having brought us east so we could come into Toledo on an angle to the regular route and take the waves on the bow rather than the quarter. This stabilized the roll, but he still did not look like a happy man. Thinking that I'd come in at a bad time, I was about to leave when he commented, "Our LORAN is out, so I'm steering magnetic, but this wind is really pushing us around."

LORAN, the radio navigation system that was the standard aid to marine and aeronautical navigation before the advent of satellite navigation systems, was extremely accurate in the Great Lakes at that time and the standard method of following courses, particularly in heavy weather.

"Is there anything I can do to help?" I asked.

"Yes," he said gladly. "Take these and look for Toledo Harbor light."

He handed me a pair of heavy marine binoculars and showed me the light on the chart, together with the description of its alternating red and white beam. We rode on in silence for quite a while; he eyed the compass and the anemometer, while I searched the gray horizon before us for a light. Finally, after nearly a quarter of an hour, I saw it: a weak red spark followed several seconds later by a white. It was slightly to port of our bow, but, as we were crabbing against the waves, we were right on course for it. I showed the light to the captain, who seemed quite happy that his dead-reckoning navigation had worked so well.

Within twenty minutes we had passed the stolid, square structure of the Toledo light, with its steep slate roof stained white by the ubiquitous gulls, and entered the gentler confines of Maumee Bay. We passed ranks of mothballed lake freighters and then entered the Maumee River, where we hove to at the dock of a four-star hotel on the Toledo waterfront. My fellow passengers and I departed; most of them had the pasty, haggard look of men who'd been through a long winter's war.

I was certainly among the better-rested of our group when we assembled at dawn for the drive down to the racecourse. The purpose of the trip was to give us a chance to sample the company's upcoming fall model lineup. On the way down to the track, we would drive the trucks, going in a caravan and stopping every fifteen or twenty minutes to switch vehicles before moving on. Then, on arrival at Mid-Ohio, we would have lunch and sit through a safety briefing before trying the company's passenger-car lineup on the track.

Like most of the writers in attendance, I saw the trucks primarily as transportation to the track; there is only so much you are going to be able to tell about a pickup or a four-by-four on smooth, paved roads at highway speeds. Still, it was a beautiful morning for a drive, with the sun out and the sky blue, the clouds and rain of the previous evening nothing now but a memory. So, adding my overnight bag to the small mountain of writers' luggage awaiting pickup in the hotel lobby, I tugged on the company-logoed ball cap that has become standard dress for these outings, went outside, and found a truck without a driver.

Our route south avoided interstates for the most part, following state roads and secondary highways on which our frequent pull-offs for driver changes would not be a problem. Rotating with my fellow writers, I worked my way up through the caravan of trucks. At some stops, if the truck I moved up to was a brand-new or unusual model, it would have an engineer in the passenger's seat to explain the various features. Other trucks, which were mostly carryovers from the previous year, would simply contain a press kit noting significant changes.

It was late in the morning when, during a stop at a roadside park, I moved up to a compact van that looked decidedly different from its peers in the caravan. It sat slightly closer to the ground, with ground-effects spoilers that reached down even further; the tires—wide, low-profile models that I would have expected to find on a sports car—were mounted on light alloy wheels, and the paint scheme featured bold racing stripes.

As we pulled back out onto the highway, the engineer in the passenger's seat explained that it was a limited-edition model with a high-performance handling package.

"We've got some twisting, turning country road coming up in the next few miles," he said. "Go ahead and see what it can do."

Although my only competitive driving has consisted of road rallies and the occasional gymkhana, I've had the good fortune over the years to get first-hand driving advice from some very skilled professionals. I crewed one season with Guldstrand Engineering as they campaigned a Z28 Camaro on the SCCA Showroom Stock Enduro circuit, and several of Dick Guldstrand's drivers had allowed me to take practice laps with them during testing, giving me pointers on performance and handling. Later, I'd also crewed with Morrison-Cook racing, and Jim Cook, one of the team owners and co-drivers, had put me in their Z51 Corvette during testing, coaching me from the passenger's seat and over the radio.

And I especially remember a morning I spent driving the handling course at the General Motors Proving Grounds with Richard Petty. Full of my minimal knowledge, I had tossed the car—a high-performance Pontiac—from corner to corner; then Petty had driven the same course, taking us through so smoothly that you would have sworn he was driving to church but turning in a time several seconds below mine. Chuckling, he had then talked me through the same course, showing me how to use brakes to compress the car's suspension coming into a corner, how to judge a turn's apex and upshift as I passed it, and how to pace my exits so I would be set up for the next turn.

Some of the knowledge I gained from these men was purely for the racetrack. Jim Cook was, for instance, the first one to tell me how to handle the situation when another vehicle spun on the track ahead of me.

"Remember, the car that's spinning is ahead of you, and distance is time on a race track," he'd told me. "A car that's spinning will eventually slow and catch. When it does, it will almost always end up darting off to one side or the other, and, if you try to dodge, you'll have a fifty-fifty chance of getting hit. So the rule is that you aim at a spinning car, knowing that it will be gone by the time you get there."

But much of what these men had taught me was usable in spirited driving at highway speeds, and I tried some of it on this new van, taking the first few turns cautiously and getting the feel of the stiffer suspension and a slight amount of oversteer—a characteristic that required the driver to physically straighten the wheel coming out of the turns rather than letting the van recover on its own.

Finally, when I had a good feel for it, I took the van briskly into a corner.

People unaccustomed to high-performance driving are often alarmed when they first experience it. A high amount of lateral G-force—feeling pushed or thrown to one side of the car—is apt to be generated. As a result, not only are the vehicle's occupants feeling that force, but the car does as well. Tires scream as they creep sideways across the pavement, and the rear tires of the vehicle—which track inside the front wheels in a normal turn—are liable to track either right behind the front tires or even outside of them.

A vehicle being operated at the upper limits of control is, in other words, likely to feel out of control to the uninitiated, and the van yawed—crabbed slightly nose-in through the turn—and squatted on the outboard front suspension as we passed the turn's apex. Finally, as I set the vehicle up for the straightaway ahead of us, I heard and felt a muted thump at the right rear corner of the van—it was the inboard rear tire, coming back down onto the pavement, as we'd taken the turn on three wheels.

It was fun, but this wasn't my van.

"I'm sorry," I said sheepishly. "I'll tone it down a bit."

"No—please—don't," the engineer responded enthusiastically. "You're the first person all morning who's really wanted to drive this. Everybody else seems under the weather or something. Please—wring it out—I'd love to hear what you think."

I was happy to oblige. With deserted blacktop road all the way to the racetrack, I took us briskly through turn after turn, slowing down on the straightaways to keep us at a legal speed but quickly losing the rest of the caravan as we took each corner aggressively. My engineer friend got out a notebook and asked me questions as I drove, and I commented and made some suggestions: modify the brake valving so the front brakes would engage just a touch earlier, stiffen the front springs to make it more difficult to bottom the suspension, and reduce the steering ratio slightly so less movement was required to go from lock to lock.

By the time we got to Lexington and the track, we were both delighted. I was, the engineer told me, the kind of driver he'd been hoping for all day. As for me—the drive had been exhilarating, but I'd had to keep the speeds low, as we'd been on public roads.

That would not be the case on the track. I'd had my appetizer, and now I was ready for the main course.

Before that could come, we'd had lunch in a tent set up in the paddock area for that purpose, and then the track steward had given us a briefing. He went through the abbreviated set of flag signals that the safety crews would be using as we drove—a green flag for an open course with no restrictions, yellow for caution, red to close the course, and black to tell a specific driver to return to the pits.

That done, we'd all grabbed our helmets and headed out to pit road. And that was where I met this new engineer at the Corvette.

Even with the seat lowered all the way, I knew that I would not be able to put my helmet on until I got into the car; the inside of the Corvette was more cockpit than interior. I did this, noting that, even though this was the slightly changed newer model of the car Morrison-Cook campaigned during the race season, I had a little more headroom than I did in the race car, which was equipped with a regulations-mandated roll cage. Putting on the seat belt, I snugged it tight and then hit the "cinch" button that would keep it that way throughout our drive. Then I started us up and took us out on the course.

The corner workers had yellow flags displayed all around the course, which was just as well since, even though I had driven at Mid-Ohio before, I wanted to re-familiarize myself before taking it at speed. Keeping my shifts at low RPMs to allow the engine and transmission to warm gradually, I weaved back and forth down the straightaways, warming up the cold tires, going under the pedestrian bridge, down a straight section and then into a hairpin turn, where I noted that the track steward had helpfully marked the apex with an orange cone. Then it was back up another straight, through some chicanes, and up a hill.

This hill was something I first remembered reading about in my teen years. It crested sharply, after which the track fell away into a corner. Roger Penske's extraordinarily versatile driver, Mark Donohue, had made it famous in his Camaro, taking the hill flat-out and putting all four tires into the air as he came over the crest, matching his shift so he would kiss the high-performance car back onto the roadway just in time to carve it into the sweeping right-hand turn. For a long time, I'd kept a magazine photo of Donohue coming off the hilltop, daylight clearly visible under all of his wheels.

We, of course, did nothing of the sort during this warm-up lap. I noted the condition of the turn—clean, with no gravel that could break traction and no shadows that might hold moisture—and then took us on, through the rest of the course, around the famous "Carousel," past the track-side pagoda, and on to the start-finish line, immediately across from pit road.

The green flag was out as I passed under the starter's stand, and, although I picked up our speed a bit, I still drove conservatively, allowing several other writers to pass me in the straights. This time, the Jump Turn felt a little bit more like a roller-coaster ride, but we still kept all four wheels firmly on the ground. My new engineer friend was enjoying the ride, and we kept up a conversation, talking loudly so we could hear one another through the helmets, chatting about the merits of our respective jobs.

As we made our second pass through the Carousel, I was satisfied with everything I'd seen. The track was clean and dry, conditions perfect. As soon as I saw the green flag being displayed from the starter's stand, I put the accelerator all the way to the floor, and my engineer passenger fell silent.

By waiting, I'd gotten clear track ahead of me, and I took advantage of it, noting that the digital speedometer quickly jumped into triple digits on the straights and entering the hairpin turn wide so I could make the apex as late as possible. I was closing quickly on a Camaro now, a red car being driven with more zeal than skill, its driver making the beginner's mistake of trying to enter every corner low and fishtailing on the way out as a result. He had the horsepower for the straightaways, though, and he was into the chicane and up and over the hill before I could pass him.

I took the hill under acceleration, unable to stifle my grin as I felt the wheels leave the ground, and dropped my RPMs to keep the engine from over-revving. I was throttling up to match wheel speed to road speed as our nose dropped, and the car was just touching down when I saw it—the driver of the Camaro ahead of us had overcorrected for the upcoming right-hand turn and lost his grip on the road.

His dark headlights and illuminated brake lights winked in my windshield like the speeded-up film of a lighthouse's revolving beacon. He was spinning down the middle of the road, and we were bearing down squarely on him.

"Distance is time"—I could almost hear Jim Cook's voice in my head—"It will be gone by the time you get there."

I aimed the Corvette's low-swept nose at the center of the spinning Camaro and kept my foot off the brake.

Sixty feet. We were closing quickly.

Fifty feet. The Camaro's spin was beginning to slow.

Forty feet. I caught a glimpse of a waving yellow flag—the corner workers, trying to warn drivers behind us.

Thirty feet. My passenger uttered a startled groan, and I saw movement from the corner of my eye. His hand . . . he was reaching for the steering wheel.

With only twenty feet between us and the spinning Camaro, I kept the steering wheel locked straight ahead with my left hand and grabbed the engineer's wrist with my right, keeping him at bay.

Ten feet. The Camaro was now sliding, barely turning.

And then, just as impact appeared imminent, the red sports coupe shot off backwards to the outside of the track, our two front bumpers missing by a matter of inches. I released the engineer's wrist and downshifted, slid into the turn a little hotter than I would have liked, and then made a quick correction and upshifted. Behind us, the track was a confusion of dust clouds and waving yellow flags as the Camaro bounced over the gravel shoulder and onto the trackside grass.

We completed the rest of the lap in the clear, drifting around the Carousel with all four tires howling. I pulled low on the finish-line straight, downshifted to scrub off the speed, and turned smartly onto pit road. As I pulled into the last pit box, the air around us was redolent with the hot-rubber smell of warmed tires.

Not wanting to embarrass my passenger, I said nothing about his grab for the steering wheel. Shifting into neutral, I pulled up on the center-console handle to set the parking brake.

"Your turn," I smiled, ready to keep my end of the deal.

"N-no," the engineer stammered. "I . . . I don't ever want to do anything like that again."

I turned and looked. The man was white as a sheet.

"Have you ever been on a race track before?" I asked him quietly.

He shook his head.

"But . . . you're an engineer for an auto company."

He looked at me blankly, and I mentioned the name of the engineer who'd ridden with me that morning, the one who'd encouraged me to "wring it out."

"Oh—him," the man in the passenger's seat nodded, understanding. "He's a suspension engineer. They spend half their time on the tracks, taking the cars through handling evaluations. They see this sort of stuff all the time. I'm a powertrain engineer on the sedan lines. I work on camshafts. I spend most of my time around engines on dynamometers. The only driving I do is on highways."

"Are you sure you wouldn't like to try a lap or two?" I asked him.

"Thanks—you did fine, but right now, I think I'd like to just go sit down for a while."

He walked off, helmet in hand, and I gave up the Corvette to some waiting writers, moving back to the next car in line. I drove most of the rest of the afternoon by myself, the one exception being when the director of Chevrolet Public Relations asked if I would take a cameraman from their video department out for a quick lap, so he could shoot some footage to be shown later at that evening's dinner.

I did that, but I did it in a five-passenger coupe, and I put the cameraman in the backseat. That would give him a better shot of the gauges, I explained.

I didn't add that it would keep him safely out of reach of the steering wheel.

In Matthew 16:21, Jesus reveals to His disciples that the time has come for Him to go to Jerusalem, suffer abuse at the hands of the religious authorities, and be put to death on the cross. In the next verse, Peter objects, saying such a thing could never be allowed. And Jesus responds (Matthew 16:23) very strongly to Peter's well-intentioned words, using the same phrase He used with the very devil in the wilderness (Luke 4:8): "Get . . . behind me, Satan."

Why the retort? Because Peter made a very common mistake, one so common that Christians still make it time and time again today. He recognized Jesus as a beloved friend, a mentor, a master, and a lord, but in his closeness and his compassion, he overlooked one very critical fact—that Jesus is also God.

As God, Jesus carries with Him several immutable qualities, one of which is the quality of prescience—or the ability to see and know in detail things yet to take place. Jesus, as God, also has the ability to preordain, or to command, future events. And the event He predicted to His apostles—His suffering and death—was a necessary sacrifice, decided by God long before man was ever created. God knew then that only His personal assumption of the debt could redeem us from the horrible consequences of sin. And when Peter speaks out against the coming of this event, Jesus, in effect, is telling him, "Be quiet; you don't know what you're talking about."

If we examine our lives honestly, we will find many times in which we—even though we are trying hard to live the Christian life—don't know what we are talking about. Like my passenger on the racetrack, we panic or try to take control, doing something we would never consider if we knew how things were actually going to turn out.

We don't get the job, the promotion, the position we were hoping for, and we are plunged into despair, never seeing at the time that God has something much better waiting for us just around the corner. We fall ill, a family member passes away, or we are deeply wounded by someone we love, and we feel that God has turned His back on us. We don't understand that this trial is going to temper us and make us a better person, equipping us to deal with a circumstance that we have yet to suspect, let alone encounter. We find ourselves in a dead end, never realizing that, just as Moses had to go in exile to the land of Midian to be prepared to speak for God and lead Israel to freedom, we are sometimes put into our own personal exile, to prepare us for a work that we don't even know is coming.

My racing friends taught me an important lesson—that what seems to be about to happen and what actually is about to transpire are often two completely different things. Pointing a car toward another vehicle spinning on a track is an unmitigated act of faith . . . faith that, by the time you have covered the intervening distance, the obstacle will no longer be there. I had that faith, because I had been prepared, but my engineer passenger did not.

In a way, I think he probably had much in common with the people of Israel when they were camped near Pihahiroth, on the edge of the Red Sea. They had just left Egypt willingly with Moses, and yet, when they saw that Pharaoh and his army were in pursuit of them, they panicked, blaming Moses for their plight and exclaiming that they were all about to die (Exodus 14:11–12).

Indeed, that must have been how it seemed—they were backed up against the sea, facing a trained army of battle-hardened troops. And yet God had directed Moses to camp there (Exodus 14:2), because God knew what none of the Israelites could know—that He had a plan to both rescue them and eliminate their antagonists.

Exodus 14:19–30 tells the story of how God raised a cloud between the Israelites and the Egyptians—a cloud that brought light and comfort to the people of Israel but darkness and confusion to the Egyptians. And then, as the cloud stood guard all that night, God made a great wind to blow out of the east, dividing the Red Sea, piling the waters into walls on either side and creating a path of dry ground on which the Israelites could make their escape. Only after they had crossed did the Lord allow Pharaoh's army to follow, and then, when the Egyptians were all far from shore, God closed the sea and let the waters consume them.

God is a god of deliverance—always has been, and always will be. And the odd thing is that, even after we have been rescued by God . . . even after He has intervened in our lives in a fashion that we could neither have predicted or imagined, we are still often hesitant to place our future dilemmas in His hands.

We can see that this is part of our inherently weak human nature in Exodus 7:14–12:51. This part of the Bible tells how God performed ten separate miracles on behalf of the Israelites before they ever got to the Red Sea. When Pharaoh refused to allow the nation of Israel to leave Egypt, God changed the Nile to a river of blood; sent plagues of frogs, lice and flies; unleashed epidemic disease that affected only the livestock of the Egyptians but left that of the Israelites untouched; afflicted the Egyptians with boils; sent a violent storm of hail; turned loose locusts that devoured the Egyptians' crops; and sent a darkness that affected only the places where the Egyptians lived but left light in the Hebrew dwellings. And then, when none of these had convinced Pharaoh to give the Israelites their freedom, God moved through the land, killing the firstborn of every Egyptian household, both man and beast, but sparing the blood-marked Hebrew households.

But even after all of these miracles—the last of which is still celebrated in the Passover feast today—God's people still doubted when they were face-to-face with imminent destruction.

Again, it all boils down, as do so many spiritual matters, to a question of faith.

"Now faith," says Hebrews 11:1, "is the substance of things hoped for, the evidence of things not seen."

And faith is the difference between fear and wonder.

The Bible tells the story of Shadrach, Meshach, and Abednego (Daniel 2:49–3:25), three Israelites who became trusted envoys of the king of Babylon. But when they refused to worship the golden idol that the king had constructed, he ordered them to be burned to death. On the day of their execution, however, even though the fire was so hot that it consumed those who threw them in, the three Israelites were able to walk unsinged in the midst of the flames, and, although only three had been tossed in, the king himself noted (Daniel 3:25), "I see four men loose, walking in the midst of the fire, and they have no hurt; and the form of the fourth is like the Son of God."

Likewise, the prophet Daniel was placed into a pit full of lions (Daniel 6:1–23) after violating a royal edict outlawing the worship of the one true God. But, this time, both Darius—the king who ordered the punishment—and Daniel had faith in God's ability to protect his children. And, sure enough, when morning came, Daniel was unharmed.

It's little wonder, then, that when a pastor friend of mine is counseling people who have finally reached a point where their backs are against the wall and they are unable to do anything to help themselves, he always surprises them by saying, "This is exciting; now we get to see what God is going to do about it."

In Jesus Christ's Sermon on the Mount, He noted (Matthew 7:7–11 and Luke 11:9–13) that even human beings, who are inherently sinful, will take pains to give their children what they need. "If ye then, being evil, know how to give good gifts unto your children," asks Jesus in Matthew 7:11, "how much more *shall your Father which is in heaven give good things to them that ask him?"*

And like a good parent who always gives a child what he or she asks for when the request is sound—a glass of water when thirsty, an extra blanket when cold—God will often answer our prayers literally, particularly when the request is one that will help us to spread the good news of Jesus Christ. But, just as a human parent will sometimes modify a request—a book instead of a toy as a gift, or cereal rather than cotton candy for break-fast—God will often answer our prayers in ways we have not ex-pected and sometimes in ways that seem, to our nearsighted per-spective, not to have addressed our prayers at all.

"Do you remember when you were a new Christian," I once asked an evangelist friend, "and you were sometimes almost afraid to ask for things in prayer, because everything you asked for was given to you?"

"Yes!" he exclaimed. And in conversations with Christians, I have found this to be true time and time again—when we are still new in our belief and just beginning to grow in our faith, God's conversations with us are often very literal. We ask for a specific position at work, and He gives it to us. We ask for finan-cial relief in some matter, and it comes almost immediately.

But, as we grow in our faith, God begins to mold us and use us. And one way He does this is by opening and closing doors in our prayer requests. We want to live in a certain part of the coun-try, but He sends us somewhere else—where our set of gifts matches perfectly a need in a church or a ministry. We pray that a sick engine on an automobile will make it to the next exit, but He lets it die—knowing that the tow-truck driver who's coming to get us will be desperately in need of the gospel message. We ask Him to soften someone's heart toward us, but He leaves it hard—knowing that the lesson we learn by dealing with that adversity in a forgiving manner will help us to grow in our Christian life.

In a letter written by the apostle Paul from Ephesus to the Chris-tian church in Corinth—a letter preserved in the Bible as 1 Corinthians—Paul shows his understanding of this, telling his

144

church members (1 Corinthians 3:2) that, as a man of God, he has fed them to this point "with milk, and not with meat, for hitherto ye were not able to bear it."

As we grow as Christians, as we pass from infancy to maturity in our spiritual lives, we begin to learn that the best thing we can ask of God in our prayer life is not for Him to give us some thing we desire, or to do some specific act that we have requested, but rather to ask of Him, as Jesus does in the model prayer He teaches in Matthew 6:10 and Luke 11:2, "thy will be done." In other words, rather than asking God to do something for us, we ask Him to help us remove those obstacles that keep Him from doing what He knows is best.

Spiritually, none of us are very tall creatures. We can only see the tiniest fraction of that which is visible from the Divine perspective. And there are times when, even though we have taken pains to remove all the obstacles between us and our heavenly Father, our prayers seem to come back unheard. A sick or injured child dies, despite our fervent appeal. Our employment ends and the bills pile up, with no relief in sight. Family problems mount, even though we are spending hours in prayerful supplication.

When these things happen, we need to remember that the Friend, the Mentor, the Provider, and Benefactor to whom we are talking is more than all of that. He is perfect. He is holy. He is God. And He will give us, not what we think is best for us, but what He knows to be necessary and knows to be right.

And in times like this, we need to learn to trust Him.

We need to learn to resist the temptation to make that lunge for the steering wheel.

After all, He's the only One who truly knows what will be there when we get farther down the track.

THE FULL SPIN

Though I walk in the midst of trouble, thou wilt revive me: thou shalt stretch forth thine hand against the wrath of mine enemies, and thy right hand shall save me.

PSALM 138:7

I still remember the sign I used to see as I passed the small grass-strip airport off the highway near my home.

"In your heart," the plain black script announced, "you've always wanted to learn how to fly."

I don't know how they knew that about me. I just know that it was right.

From the time I learned to read, I devoured books on airplanes. My first book was the one with which my grandmother taught me to read—the Bible—but the second was a book to which my father had contributed a photograph: *A History of Marine Corps Aviation in World War II.*

147

There were no VCRs or DVD players in the years when I was a child, but I would scour the television listings every weekend, checking to see if *The Spirit of St. Louis* or *The Flying Leathernecks* was playing on the matinee broadcasts out of Chicago. When I visited my aunt and uncle, they knew that the easiest way to entertain me was to take me to the county airport and let me watch the weekend pilots practicing their touch-and-goes on the narrow concrete strip.

And the high point of one summer was when I looked up and saw an old Dauntless dive-bomber sputtering over the house, black smoke puffing out in oily dashes behind it. We jumped in my uncle's battered Willys Jeep and raced down a gravel road to where the Dauntless had slid to a wheels-up landing in a bean field, its leather-jacketed pilot climbing out and surprisingly calm about the whole thing. He had bought the old warbird at a military surplus sale in Ohio and was ferrying it back to Iowa when the engine had given out. I remember the power the old military airplane had exuded, even with its propeller bent and uprooted bean plants stuck in its perforated air-brake panels. And I remember the wonderful mechanical smell of it and the lanky, laid-back attitude of its pilot, and I knew right away that this was what I wanted to do when I grew up— although I hoped I would make more stylish landings.

I reached adulthood without realizing that dream. Two of the colleges I attended taught flying, but, although scholarships and fellowships would have taken care of the tuition, the costs of airplane rentals and aviation fuel—called "lab fees" in the college-catalog lexicon—were hopelessly beyond me. And then, after my university degrees were *faits accompli* on my office walls, the time required for flying lessons and ground schools seemed always to escape me.

There were other excuses. Student flying is done under strict visual flight rules, with work in and above clouds absolutely out of the question. But I have lived all of my life in the Midwest, where the weather is notoriously fickle.

And flying is not a skill one wants to learn in fits and starts—you either stick with it, or start over time and time again.

Still, I treasured the time I spent in friends' airplanes, even if it was in the right-hand seat. Al Lee, the writer and educator with whom I'd become firm friends in graduate school, had been flying for years, owning in succession a Piper Tri-Pacer, an Ercoupe, a Piper Colt, a Cherokee 180, a twin-engine Seneca, a Piper Comanche, another Cherokee 180, and a sliding-canopied Yankee. He and I flew to Louisville together in the Seneca when we'd both had separate writing assignments there and, on the way back, I'd flown the plane from takeoff to final approach, relinquishing the controls five hundred feet from the runway so Al—the pilot in command—could land it. He'd commented then that I seemed to have a natural talent for flying, and he'd urged me to take lessons and, in the jargon of flying, "get my ticket." But the excuses mounted, and I did not follow through.

It was Al, though, who finally convinced me to take the plunge. He called me late one spring when I was doing publicity writing and marketing work for one of the auto companies. We talked about schedules, and I mentioned that I had been working overtime doing the support work on a new truck that would be coming out in May. Then I added that I had a fairly light summer planned, having done enough work during the spring to earn my retainer through August.

"That's great," Al said. And then he explained why.

I had known Al's son, Cal, since he was a kid towing a lawn mower behind his bicycle from yard-job to yard-job. As the son of an airplane owner, Cal had, naturally, earned his private pilot's license as soon as he was old enough, and he had gone on to earn certifications as both a commercial pilot and an instructor with ratings in single-engine airplanes, multi-engine airplanes, and even seaplanes. Not that he was planning to teach flying for a career—he was just finishing a bachelor's with honors in philosophy from a prestigious Michigan university.

Still not certain what career path he wanted to follow, Cal took a job as a flight instructor at a suburban airport. Now he was trying to fill up his student roster, and Al naturally remembered me as a prospect.

I didn't even tell Al I'd have to think about it. This wasn't coddling myself with expensive lessons in a skill that I probably didn't really need; this was a noble effort to help out the son of a friend. Never mind that I had wanted to do it all my life.

Two minutes after I hung up with Al, I'd called Cal at the airport and scheduled my first lesson. We'd meet at 9:00 the following morning.

Cal began our lesson with a preflight inspection of the aircraft, a Cessna 172. As I'd often helped his father preflight their various aircraft, I didn't need much instruction in this, and we chatted as I checked the ailerons and flaps, the empennage (tail) and its control surfaces, the antennae attachment points, and the landing gear, looking for loose rivets or wrinkles on the fuselage as we went. The Cessna, like most airplanes, carries its fuel in its wings and, while I'd not operated a high-wing aircraft before, the fuel drains were easy to find, and I siphoned a bit of fuel out of each wing and then checked it for contamination. Then I pulled over a ladder to visually check the fuel levels through the wing-top filler openings.

When I got to the engine, Cal showed me where to find the fuel drain there, and I expelled a bit of avgas and checked the oil. We checked the propeller for nicks or signs of a damaged seal, walked around to insure that the pitot tube (which measures airflow for wind speed) and the static port (which provides ambient air pressure to the instruments) were clear, and lifted the vane in the stall-indicator mechanism, to make sure the warning horn sounded in the cockpit.

With that done and the aircraft untied, we were ready to get in and start the engine. Most small, single-engine airplanes are very similar in this respect, and it only took Cal a few minutes to show me the Cessna's idiosyncrasies. I gave the primer pump its four strokes, pulled the throttle out to about a quarter-inch from full idle, turned on the master switch and both magnetos, and cranked the starter for just a moment before the engine caught and the propeller became a transparent disk in front of us. We donned our headsets, checked the intercom and radios, and began to taxi out.

Driving a car is, for most of us, so common an activity that it has become nothing more than a background to transportation—getting from one place to another with little thought to the method. For me, I'm happy to say, flight has always been an event. I like the conscientious ritual of running the engine up to full power, checking for oil pressure, switching off each magneto independently to simulate a failure, and running the controls to full stop to check for obstructions. The whole procedure has a nearly military methodicalness that I admire; it just feels as if one is getting ready to *do* something.

And we were. After I'd done the run-up to our satisfaction, I got on the radio and announced our departure and then, with a quick check for incoming traffic, turned onto the runway, verified that the autogyro and the compass were still in agreement and flipped on the altitude-encoding transponder and the landing light. With my right hand holding the throttle all the way in for full power, I released the brakes and sent us hurtling down the asphalt strip.

There is a wonderful paradox to flying. To the observer on the ground, the whole business on the taxiway and in the run-up area—the visual inspections, the checks, the lists, and radio clearances—may all just seem like boring minutia compared to the exhilaration of takeoff.

And while it is certainly true that there is a thrill to leaving the ground, the truth is that all of the preflight routines and the business of working the radio require such concentration—especially if one is departing into a high-traffic area, with airplanes behind you, waiting to depart—that the actual takeoff is something of a relief. It is as if one is busy, busy, busy—and then flying. And though it might not seem so outside, the tempo inside the cockpit slows a perceptible click once one is actually airborne.

Cal asked me to make a standard right turn once we had reached a safe altitude, and I did, picking up a compliment from him on the way I coordinated the controls, putting in enough rudder to keep us from skidding, and keeping the nose slightly up so we did not lose altitude as we turned. From a layman's point of view, I already knew how to fly—that is, how to turn, climb, descend, and cruise in level flight. In fact, there were some things I did extremely well. Both Cal's father and at least one other pilot had noted that, having worked with and around engines since I was a teenager and being able to recognize the notes of engines working even a few RPMs apart, I had the knack for synchronizing the throttles on a twin-engine airplane, working by ear alone and not even looking at the gauges.

But learning to fly is more than learning to take the plane up in the air and then bring it down again. True, I had made several flights—in fact, I probably had several hours of flying time under my belt. But those had all been routine trips, in which little precision maneuvering had been involved and—more importantly—nothing significant had gone wrong. Part of learning to become a pilot is learning how an airplane can become unstable, understanding how to avoid those conditions, and mastering the techniques for bringing an airplane back under control once it has gotten out of hand.

After taking me through a few gentle turns and ascertaining that I could trim the airplane and keep it in level flight, Cal introduced me to one of the most common de-nominators in private-aviation accidents—the stall.

If, as a child, you ever stuck your hand out of the window of a moving vehicle, two things probably happened.

The most likely, of course, is that a parent or some other adult told you to pull your hand back inside.

But in the intervening second, you probably noticed that your hand produced different effects as you varied its angle in the airstream moving past the car. If you angled it down, the wind pushed it down. Angled up, it rose. And if you cupped your hand slightly, even if you kept it relatively level, it would feel light, almost weightless.

The effect you were feeling was the result of differences in air pressure above and below your hand. With your hand slightly cupped, the air moving across the top of your hand had to travel slightly farther in the same amount of time—because it was following a curved surface—than that moving across your palm. As a result, the area of air pressure just above your hand was lower than that below, and that produced *lift*, making your hand feel lighter, as if some unseen force was buoying it up . . . which it was.

Airplane wings operate on the same principle. While some of an airplane's lift comes from the air wedging under a wing as it moves, most of the force that keeps an airplane airborne is lift resulting from the differences in air pressure above and below the wings.

Back to the car—if no adult was attentive enough to stop you before you could experiment further, you may have angled your hand upward further and further and noticed something strange. While a slight upward angle made your hand rise in the airstream, an acute angle did not necessarily make it rise even more. In fact, at some point, your hand would stop rising, even though you were holding your open palm to the oncoming air, and your hand would begin to drop back down.

Whether you were aware of it or not, that childhood experiment acquainted you with the basis of the aeronautic stall.

Automobiles stall when their engines quit running. But an airplane stalls when its wings stop flying—stop producing lift.

When a wing—an airplane's wing, a bird's wing, or a six-year-old's hand sticking out a car window—is angled too far upward, the air going across the top of it does not travel all the way across the curve. Instead, it only follows part of the curved surface before breaking up into vertices. As a result, less and less of the surface is producing lift and, when the weight of the aircraft (or bird, or hand) exceeds the lifting power of the remaining wing surface, the airplane will begin to drop.

This is of concern to pilots because wings stall more easily when the airplane is moving slowly (the air travels over the wing at a lower velocity, producing less lift), or when the airplane is pulling out of a dive or making a banked turn (the centrifugal force created by the flight path—the same force that presses you down in your seat when you're in an airplane making such a maneuver—increases the amount of lift necessary to keep the airplane flying).

The two events during which a pilot is most at risk of stalling an airplane, Cal explained, are takeoff and landing. Takeoffs involve a relatively steep climb to altitude—a climb that takes the wings to a steep angle of attack relative to the oncoming air (much like the six-year-old's hand canted up). And one cannot land an airplane properly without coming very close to its stall threshold—in fact, in a perfect landing, the airplane should stall and stop flying just a split-second before its wheels touch the ground.

A quarter of all private-aviation accidents involve stalls, Cal told me, and most of those occur while leaving, or returning to, the ground. That being the case, he wanted to make me very familiar with the sensation of an oncoming stall . . . but we'd do so under circumstances that would take the ground out of the equation. He asked me to take us to two thousand feet above ground level—high enough to give us plenty of sky with which to work.

First we performed a couple of "clearing turns"—circling lazily to get a complete view of the surrounding sky, so we could check for any other traffic. Then, following Cal's instructions, I set up for a power-on stall by going through the steps a pilot might follow in preparing to take off. We reduced our power to 1,500 RPM and slowly reduced our speed to just above rotation speed—the speed at which the front wheel lifts from the ground during takeoff. Cal then asked me to give the airplane full throttle, pulling the yoke back farther and farther until the stall-warning horn began to sound and a buffeting shook the entire airplane. At this point I could feel the torque and the P-factor—a force created by propwash spiraling around the airplane and striking the left surface of the horizontal stabilizer, or tail-fin—yawing the airplane to the left, so I applied some right rudder and, at Cal's request, kept pulling the yoke back toward my chest.

Extremely high-performance airplanes, such as the ones sometimes seen in air shows, can hang in the air on the power of their turning propellers alone, much as a helicopter can hover using its rotors. But light utility aircraft, particularly the modestly powered airplanes used for training, cannot. Even with the engine roaring at full throttle, we passed through the prestall buffet, felt momentarily light as we began to drop, and then nosed over as gravity tugged on the heaviest part of the airplane—the engine.

The cabin darkened as our wings blocked out the early morning sun. Cornfields, bright green with black lines of shadow scribed between the rows, filled every inch of the windscreen.

"Okay," Cal said, speaking calmly, as if this were an everyday occurrence—which, for him, it was. "Keep your hands on the yoke, but release the pressure. Good. We're already at full throttle, so you have all the power you need. Just pull back gently . . . not too fast, or we'll stall again, but fast enough to keep from losing too much altitude. Okay, we're returning to level flight. Reduce your throttle to cruising speed."

I did as he said. The cornfields slid back under us, where they belonged, brilliant blue horizon edged in from the top of the windscreen, and we were flying again. But our altimeter showed that we had lost more than three hundred feet on our recovery.

"The moral here," Cal said, "is that, if you do that too close to the ground, like right after takeoff, you won't have enough room to recover."

Then he had me do a slow, spiraling climb back to two thousand feet above ground level, giving me ample time to look again for other traffic, and to absorb the fact that, even with its engine roaring under full power, there were certain conditions under which our little airplane simply could not fly.

Back at altitude, Cal took the controls and explained that, on final approach to an airstrip, power to the engine is generally reduced to idle shortly before the airplane crosses the runway threshold, and the aircraft simply glides in for a landing.

This allows the pilot to land in the shortest possible distance, but it also reduces flying speed and thins the margin between flight and stall.

Cal reduced our speed in three steps, each time lowering the flaps and increasing the cup to the underside of the wings. Finally, when full flaps had been introduced, he pulled all the way back on the throttle, reducing the engine to an idle.

Still keeping his hand at the ready on the throttle, Cal pulled back gradually on the yoke, raising the nose to keep us at altitude.

Small airplanes, with their slightly muffled engines and thin fuselages, are notoriously noisy, but ours had become ominously quiet. The engine's roar was now just a mild hum through our noise-suppressing headsets, and the roar of the wind outside the cabin was now startlingly absent. The stall warning sounded, very noticeable in the quiet cockpit, and the airplane bumped just twice before flight abandoned it and we nosed over into a stall. Releasing his pressure on the yoke, Cal smoothly brought the engine back to full throttle, leveled us off, and took the flaps off in stages.

He talked through the steps he had followed as he took us back up to practice height and then, with a quiet, "Your airplane," relinquished the controls so I could try.

There is a decided roller-coaster quality to the nose-first drop of a stalling airplane and, as I've always liked such things, I found myself grinning as I reduced power, lowered the flaps, and put the little Cessna into its nose-high, slow-flight attitude. The horizon fell away and blue sky filled the windscreen, the morning sun accentuating a hundred minute scratches in the Plexiglas. Watching the altimeter, I pulled back on the yoke, and the deathly silence again began to envelop us. Almost without thinking about it, I applied some right rudder, as I had before, and the stall warning began to sound. We shuddered like a creature in a cold breeze, and then we began to sink.

But we did not nose cleanly over. The right wingtip sank first, and the airplane began to rotate, the cornfields below us heeling over like the deck of a capsizing ship. The windscreen took on a resemblance to a commercial washing machine, the fields slowly beginning to tumble upon themselves.

Even before we had made the first fraction of a revolution, I knew what had happened. My right rudder correction, which had countered the torque and P-factor during the power-on stall, had nothing against which to equalize with the engine cut back to an idle. When the airplane nosed over, the angled rudder had caused us to yaw as we dropped, which put us into an incipient spin.

Spins are dangerous. In a spinning airplane, the wing on the outside of the spin is moving faster than that on the inside. Both wings are stalled, but one stalls much more dramatically than the other. Like a single-bladed maple seed, the aircraft plummets, rotating as it falls.

I thought of all this as we began to describe a circle, like bugs being washed down a drain, and I knew that, although what we were in at the moment was only the beginnings of a spin, it would, by the time we'd completed our second revolution, be all the way into a full spin. I had just read the section on spins from the *Cessna Manual of Flight,* and I remembered what it had to say there about the full spin: "There is no guarantee that a normal category airplane will recover from a fully developed spin."

We were a little over halfway into the first rotation, the tumbling cornfields picking up speed, when I reflected on three things.

The first was that we had no parachutes on the airplane.

The second was that I couldn't remember the last time I'd updated my will.

The third was that I certainly wouldn't be doing my best friend any favors if I managed to kill his only son.

And that was when Cal asked, "Um . . . would you like me to take it, or do you want me to talk you through it?"

The strangest thing was that he sounded so calm. There we were, with wind screaming over the control surfaces and a few hundred acres of agricultural real estate revolving in the same image that I'd seen in dozens of fighter-ace movies, and Cal was asking me the question with the same tone one might use on the golf course, asking the following party if they'd like to play through.

It was, in fact, probably his tone that triggered my response. Because, even though I had just been wishing that someone, anyone, would take the controls from me and get me out of this, I found myself saying, "Sure. Talk me through."

158

"Okay," Cal said, as we got three-quarters of the way through the first revolution, still not a hint of fright or worry in his voice. "Leave the throttle at idle and don't turn the yoke. We want ailerons neutral. Good."

We completed the first revolution.

"Okay, now, flaps all the way up," Cal continued. "That's it. Good. We're spinning to the right"—*that* much I was aware of; I was on the edge of vertigo, watching rows of corn sweep like the second hand on a clock—"so we need full rudder deflection in the opposite direction. Give it full left rudder. There you go. Spin's slowing. Now release the back-pressure on your yoke. Remember, the plane wants to fly. Right. No throttle yet, gravity will give us all the airspeed we need. Okay, rotation's stopped. Neutralize the rudder; pull us out of the dive. Watch your horizon come up. There it is. Give us some throttle now. That's it. We're flying again."

And that *was* it. The whole thing probably took no more than fifteen seconds, and the only evidence I had that anything had taken place was the cornfields, now hundreds of feet closer than they had been when we'd started the spin. I thought of all the times I'd flown previously and wondered how I would have reacted had someone not been there to talk me through a procedure that was anything but intuitive.

I turned to Cal. But, before I could thank him, he was nodding.

"Let's go back up and try it again, okay?" he asked. "Just go easier on the rudder when the power's off this time, and we'll be fine."

I did.

And we were.

There is a tremendous confidence that comes with knowing that, even if we are facing a situation that we have never, ever faced before, we face it in the company of Someone who can handle anything.

The recovery of an airplane from a spin—or, for that matter, the recovery of an airplane from a stall—is not an intuitive process. When an airplane is falling, the pilot's every instinct says to pull back on the yoke . . . an action that can only exacerbate the situation. Had I been by myself when that Cessna 172 began its spin, I would very probably have ridden the aircraft to the ground, struggling all the way, but never doing what was necessary to help myself out of my situation.

But I wasn't by myself. When I dropped the Cessna into its spin, I was blessed with the company of an extraordinarily gifted instructor—one who could easily, calmly, and patiently talk me through the recovery.

Wouldn't it be wonderful if we had a wise, patient, and knowledgeable expert at our side every time we faced a problem, a dilemma, or even an unfamiliar situation in life?

The good news is that, if we are Christians, we do.

This story is about learning to fly, but I cannot think back on it without remembering another incident that took place a few years later, just as I had finished my course of instruction in cave diving.

The day that I received my certification as a cave diver, I led my first practical dive with a friend, the instructor who had certified me. Our tanks were only partially full, but they held the minimum pressure needed for starting a dive, and neither of us was keen to take the time and go get a fill. So we agreed that I would take us in until I hit two-thirds of my starting pressure, or until I felt that we should turn around, whichever came first.

We did our dive in the Madison Blue Hole cave system, and I took us past two fairly narrow restrictions and on down a passage that led to the nethermost regions of that cave. When I got to within one hundred pounds of my turn-around pressure, I could

160

see that the way ahead would be narrow and turning around where we were would be more convenient, so I gave my partner the thumbs-up "return" signal, and we made our way out.

Cave diving is, of course, a world of darkness and danger. The only air one has to breathe is the air one carries on one's back. And naturally, most newer cave divers are worried by that environment.

I would also later learn that the route I had led us on in Madison Blue Hole had claimed the lives of five divers just a year or so earlier. And, when we'd finished our decompression and ascended to the surface of the headspring, my partner was ecstatic, telling me that he had never had a newly certified cave diver go as far into such an advanced system. He remarked on my calmness and my apparent lack of fear underwater, and I told him, "Well, it's not as if I was alone down there."

"I see," my friend replied, "having me in there with you helped, eh?"

"Well," I grinned, "you, too. But you weren't the One I was referring to."

Before His ascension into heaven, Jesus promised His disciples that all who received Him as their Savior would receive a "Comforter" (John 14:16) who would help guide and guard them. That Comforter is referred to elsewhere in the Bible as the "Holy Spirit" or the "Holy Ghost," but equally valid translations of the original New Testament language would be the "Holy Life" or the "Holy Breath."

The Bible tells us that God exists in a Trinity—three Persons who are also One. There are God the Father, reigning on His heavenly throne, and God the Son, who died for our sins and was resurrected to prove that we could have eternal life. The Holy Spirit is the Third: that Person of God who chooses to reside within us when we accept Christ's gift—His willingness to make the payment for our sins—and become Christians.

To those who are new to faith, and to many who are not so new, the concept of the Holy Trinity is oftentimes difficult to even contemplate. As mere men and women, we simply have a hard time picturing a Being who is three in one.

But the fact is that there is only one God, yet there are three individuals manifest within God—individuals who not only exist simultaneously but who occupy and communicate with one another and even are the subject of one another's prayer.

In Luke 4:1, for instance, Jesus—the Second Person of God— is described as returning from Jordan "full of the Holy Ghost." Jesus prayed constantly to the First Person of God—God the Father. Not only that—in Matthew 26:39, Jesus tells the Father that He prays events will transpire "not as I will, but as thou wilt." And one of the last things Jesus said on the cross was the Aramaic phrase "Eli, Eli, lama sabachthani?" which, translated, is the opening sentence of Psalm 22: "My God, my God, why hast thou forsaken me?"

God full of God? God praying to God? God forsaking God? We will never, in this life, fully understand the nature of the Holy Trinity, simply because one cannot understand from the limited basis of human experience a relationship that exists wholly on the infinite and divine level.

But there have been many attempts to at least begin to explain the concept of God in three Persons, and my personal favorite is a comparison of the Trinity to the sun.

The sun is a star that exists in the heavens, 93 million miles distant; it is also light that is sent to us here on earth; and it is warmth that we feel upon and within ourselves. In these three qualities, we have at least partial parallels to those of God the Father in Heaven (the source), God the Son (the light), and God the Holy Spirit (the warmth and the presence). When we are flushed from being outdoors, we do not, after all, say that we were "in the light." We say that we were "in the sun." And when we talk to Jesus . . . when we listen to the Holy Spirit . . . we are talking with and listening to God Almighty, the One who identified Himself to Moses as the great "I AM" (Exodus 3:14).

Similes such as this can hint at the nature of the Holy Trinity, even though they cannot fully explain it. But that doesn't matter.

The important thing is that, when we accept the Second Person of God as our Savior, the First Person of God sends the Third to dwell within us. And that Third Person—the Holy Spirit—leads us, guides us, and communicates to us God's holy will.

My instructor was the one who gave me confidence in the airplane. But God the Spirit was the One who so calmed me in the depths of the cave. And I have learned to depend on the Holy Spirit as my unfailing Guide when I navigate life's perils.

How does one hear from God? I have never heard God speak in an audible voice, never received a note from Him or read, as the prophet Daniel did (Daniel 5:24–29), strange handwriting that appeared on the wall. I have not knowingly spoken with angels—God's messengers—although Hebrews 13:2 assures me that I may often have done so without realizing who they were.

Yet I know that He has spoken to me—that He does so, in fact, almost constantly.

In Revelation 3:7, Jesus talks about opening and shutting doors. And while the "doors" he refers to in this passage are the portals to salvation and righteousness, the fact is that God can, and will, open and shut other "doors" in our lives, as well. When I have a difficult decision to make . . . when I am faced with choices that appear unclear . . . I know that, if I put the matter in God's hands, He will clearly show me which way to go—often by eliminating the choices He does not wish me to consider.

At other times, God may communicate with an impression that is unmistakably not my own. I clearly remember driving down a busy interstate earlier this year, when I was suddenly given the strong sense that I should get off the highway at the next exit. I know that this was not my thought, because I was rushing to get to a meeting. But I obeyed, stopped at a shop to pick up a carryout cup of coffee, and suddenly again had a strong notion that I should get back on the highway.

Wondering what this was all about, I got back onto the interstate—and immediately encountered the five-car accident that had occurred just minutes earlier. God may have delayed me to keep me safe. Or He may have delayed me because He knew that

I would use my first-aid and rescue training to assist the people trapped and injured in the accident. I don't know—but I am certain that it was God I heard from that day. And this was not, in my mind, an unusual or exceptional occurrence. God speaks to His children constantly, and if we do not hear Him, the problem is usually that we are not listening.

The best way to learn to listen to God is to converse with Him. Conversation with God is prayer, and prayer is so important that the Bible records many instances of Jesus going off alone to pray to His heavenly Father.

Nor would Jesus limit His prayer to His earthly ministry. When He promised the Holy Ghost to His disciples, the words He used were (John 14:16a) "And I will pray the Father, and he shall give you another Comforter."

"Will pray"—future tense.

There are three words in the original language of the New Testament that are usually translated as "ask" or "pray." And of the three, the word used in John 14:16 is not the one that describes going to another in the greatest degree of humility—begging. But, interestingly enough, neither is it the least. In this Bible verse, Jesus clearly shows that, even though He is a Person of God and an equal, He is going to make supplicant prayer part of His life even after His resurrection and ascension into heaven.

And if prayer is so important that it takes place between the equal Persons of God, how much more important must it be for us?

1 Thessalonians 5:17 instructs us to "Pray without ceasing."

Even though this verse was written by Paul, we probably see the influence here of Luke, the physician and gospel writer who was a disciple of both Paul and Peter, because the word translated "without ceasing" was usually used in medical documents, to describe a condition (such as a cough) that does not go away. If we were to literally translate it into twenty-first century terms, we might say "pray chronically."

I believe that Paul put it this way because first-century Christians were probably little different from their peers twenty cen-

turies later. They probably tended to use prayer as a fire alarm or a letter to Santa Claus: a call for help when all else had failed and a list of requests for things and circumstances that, in most cases, they didn't need.

Supplication—asking God for blessings—is certainly part of prayer. But it is by no means the only part.

John 1:12, Romans 8:14, and a number of other places in the Bible assure us that, when we receive Jesus Christ as our Savior, we become the children of God Almighty, and He becomes our Father. And, just as any good parent delights in giving things to their children, God also takes pleasure in blessing us.

But a parent-child relationship in which the child's only communication is nonstop solicitation—continually asking, begging, nagging, even whining—is a relationship anyone would recognize as essentially flawed. God, like any parent, wants more dimension than that. He wants love, respect, tenderness, and confidence—and He gives all those things, as well.

Prayer begins with recognizing God for who He is—the Supreme Being; the Creator; the all-powerful, all-holy Lord of heaven and earth. If, as we go to God in prayer, we think about who He truly is, there is only one way we can approach Him, and that is in humility.

James 5:16 advises Christians to "confess your faults one to another" and to pray for the healing of one another's transgressions. James says this because it is important for us to urge one another to resist our natural inclination to sin (which will be with us until the day that we die) and to constantly strive for a life of repentance.

Likewise, I think it is important, when we talk with God, to acknowledge how far short we fall of His expectations each day; to express our sorrow for those shortcomings; and to acknowledge that the only reason those sins do not damn us is because Jesus has already paid for them with His redeeming blood.

At this point in prayer, we establish ourselves where we should be—humbled before God and totally dependent on His mercy. That is, I know, a tough pill to swallow in a day and age that *glorifies the individual, but Christianity is not about glorifying ourselves. It is about glorifying God.*

Having properly established our relationship to the Father, we are then ready—not to ask for things but to thank Him for what He has already given. If we look at that "pray without ceasing" verse in First Thessalonians, we see that it comes in the center of a string of verses (1 Thessalonians 5:16–18) that are all about expressing our happiness for what God has already done for us: "Rejoice evermore. Pray without ceasing. In every thing give thanks: for this is the will of God in Christ Jesus concerning you."

And they are followed with a reminder (1 Thessalonians 5:19) to keep the pipeline open to the part of God that resides within us—"Quench not the Spirit."

What do we have to thank God for? Breathe in. Breathe out. God gave that breath to you. From the sweetness of honey to the love of a spouse, we have God to thank for every moment of true joy we have ever experienced, or will ever experience, because, as the Bible says in James 1:17a, "Every good gift and every perfect gift is from above, and cometh down from the Father of lights."

If you think of it this way, the question is not what we have to thank Him for but where we could possibly stop. And if a Christian can put himself or herself in tune with this way of thinking, it's only a short step before one is really able to "in every thing" (1 Thessalonians 5:18) give thanks. You might find yourself saying things such as, "Thank you, Lord, for this traffic jam, so I can spend a quiet moment with you," or "Thank you, Lord, for allowing me to fail that class; it has given me the opportunity to examine whether I am doing what You would want me to do with my life."

Should we ask God for things? Of course we should—in a humble, contrite, and Christian way. And, if we truly acknowledge God as our Master, I don't see why we should limit the things we ask for to the big, life-changing categories. I rarely do any work—whether it's writing the words you are reading right now, or mending a leaking faucet—without asking God to help me do it well. When I talk with others about Christ, I ask Him to give me the words to witness. When I travel, I ask Him to keep me safe. When I misplace my keys, I ask Him to show me where they are.

And why shouldn't I? I know that He knows where I put them!

Will God answer prayer? In John 14:13, Jesus promises, "whatsoever ye shall ask in my name, that will I do." But I think it's important to bear that phrase—"in my name"—in mind as we read this. If we are asking for something sinful, we cannot possibly ask for it in Jesus' name. If we are asking for anything that is outside God's will for our life, then we can't ask Jesus to underwrite it. The only matters we can really be certain are in the will of God are matters that He tells us are within His will in His Holy Book.

These are usually matters of ministry. And even then, the ministry in question must be the ministry God has picked for us, not the one we have picked for ourselves.

This takes a lot of trust on our part. I have known people who have fervently prayed for things they felt were in God's will—to be spared from financial disaster, to save the life of a loved one, or to be freed from some illness or oppression—only to have God refuse the request. But, if they kept in sync with God, they would eventually realize—sometimes years or even decades later—that He had His reason for doing what He did. Feeling that he could be a better witness if he was well, the apostle Paul asked God to heal an infirmity three times (2 Corinthians 12:8). When God refused, Paul realized that God had a reason; that God's "strength is made perfect in weakness" (2 Corinthians 12:9).

Prayer opens the dialogue with God. And once that dialogue is opened, if we learn to listen, we will hear—not simply from the Supreme Authority, but also from the best Friend we will ever know.

In John 15:14, Jesus promises that, if we will commit ourselves to a Christian life, He will consider us to be His friends. Think of that for a moment. The Alpha and the Omega, the One to whom presidents and kings must bow in supplication, is not just our Lord, not just our Master, and not just our acquaintance. He is our Friend. And friends talk.

167

With God in our lives, then, we are never empty or alone. We are always in the presence of our best Friend. It would be rude—and wrong—to ignore Him. We should talk with Him. And we should listen.

And how can we be sure that what we are hearing is truly from God? I use this touchstone: If the advice I feel I am being given is in accordance with Scripture—not just suggested by a verse read out of context but in accordance with what the Bible consistently has to say on a subject—then I can be certain that God is telling me what to do. And if I feel I am hearing something not in accordance with Scripture. . . well, that's my sinful nature talking, and not God, because God is perfectly consistent and never, ever contradicts Himself.

When Jesus promised Christians the Holy Ghost in John 14:16, the word He used—the word translated as "Comforter"—was a word that literally means "One who works alongside." And when Jesus said, "another Comforter," He had reason for saying "another." You see, the first Comforter is Jesus Christ Himself.

Knowing this, we can be certain that, as Christians, there is no situation in life we will ever have to face alone. The Holy Spirit is always there with us. And so is Jesus, our Friend.

That's why I can be confident. My flight instructor knew how to help me keep a spinning airplane from crashing to the ground. And my life Instructor knows how to keep my life on a course that is safe, and right, and—most important of all—pleasing to Him.

8

THE KEEPER
OF THE WINDS

*Thou art more glorious and excellent
than the mountains of prey.*

Psalm 76:4

I first heard of Finis Mitchell in Madison, Wisconsin. My old friend Chuck Winger lived there at the time, and he'd invited me to come visit and do some rock-climbing before we made a trip out west.

For as long as I had known him, Chuck had been talking about the Wind River Range, the true rooftop of Wyoming. Covering areas of the Bridger National Wilderness, the Pope Agie and Glacier Primitive Areas, and the Wind River Indian Reservation, the Winds contain Gannett Peak—at 13,785 feet, the highest point in Wyoming, fifteen feet taller than Grand Teton, which can be seen, albeit distantly, from Gannett's summit.

Summit-bagging was, however, just one of the Wind's attractions, Chuck told me. He had done several stints there as a teen with the National Outdoor Leadership School, and he waxed eloquent about the hiking trails, the vistas, and especially the high alpine trout fishing in the Wind River Range's lakes.

Chuck and I had traveled and climbed together many times—in the Seneca Rocks region of West Virginia, the Shawangunks of New York, and smaller areas throughout Ohio and Michigan. But we had never been to the Rockies together, and Chuck assured me that my life would all have been in vain if I let it slip by without wetting a line in a Wind River lake and planting my boots atop a Wind River peak.

I had long since come to trust Chuck's recommendations. So, after turning in a few writing assignments early and arranging my schedule for a few weeks of free time, I drove to Madison, where Chuck lived at the time, and climbed with him at Devil's Lake while we bought provisions and organized the equipment for our trip.

We were planning to both fish and climb in the Winds. Actually, the fishing would be essential, as we would be carrying so much climbing gear that it would reduce the room we'd have for food. Ice axes, crampons, ice pitons, chocks, carabiners by the dozens, and several coils of kernmantle climbing rope were essential elements for the climbing we wanted to do, as were squat mountain tents, mummy bags, windsuits, down parkas, multi-fuel stoves, cooksets, glacier goggles, water bottles, fuel bottles, compasses, laminated USGS maps, backcountry first-aid kits complete with prescription pain killers and sutures, and changes of durable woolen clothing. We estimated our pack weights for Chuck and myself at close to ninety pounds apiece, without food, and Kay, Chuck's wife, would carry a sixty-pound pack, as well.

But Chuck assured me that, aside from staples such as coffee, sugar, Bisquik, cooking oil, salt, and our first-morning bacon and eggs—one of our traditions in the wilderness—we could live off the land fairly easily in the Winds. Berries would be in season, as it was late summer, and the trout, he assured me, would all but leap battered into the pan.

Twenty minutes after I arrived in Madison, Chuck and I were out on the pavement, making a training run. Early the next morning, Chuck, Kay, and I were climbing the dew-damp cliffs above Devil's Lake; we had always thought that the best training for mountaineering was high-grade rock-climbing. And through every bit of it, Chuck talked about our upcoming trip, which would include not only the Winds but Teton National Park, Yellowstone, and other areas of Wyoming and Montana. As we ate our lunch at the foot of a Devil's Lake rock climb, he handed me a dog-eared green-covered book, about the size of a wallet.

"We can get you your own copy in Pinedale, but you'll want to read this through before then," Chuck told me. "This is the best guide to the Winds."

The book was *Wind River Trails,* by Finis (rhymes with "Linus") Mitchell. I read it that evening at bedtime and was pleasantly surprised by the tone. It was not the come-out-here-if-you're-tough-enough approach I'd seen in other mountain guidebooks. The writing was kind, gentle, even welcoming. The author seemed eager to share what he called "God's great Wind River Range," and he extolled the virtues of the country, right down to the water: "so pure . . . just one drop away from heaven."

Two weeks later, I'd discovered that Chuck and the guidebook writer were right. He, Kay, and I caught all the fish we would eat at our first campsite in the Winds, a lake amid the pines. The next morning, we hiked up past the timberline to the Titcomb Valley, camped there and fished again (the ice of the Titcomb Glacier made a convenient freezer in which to store our dinner for the next day) and rose at 3:00 in the morning to get an alpine start on an ascent of Gannett.

I can still close my eyes and picture walking up the snow- and ice-covered trail to the couloir at the head of the valley, the steam of our breath rising to mingle with the bright vapor of the Milky Way, the points on the ends of our ice axes sparking bluely beneath the snow as we would plant them to steady ourselves and strike the hard granite sleeping underneath.

We chopped steps all the way up the couloir and were atop it well before sunrise. Gannett, snow-mantled and purple in the dusk, seemed close enough to touch. Crossing the Dinwoody Glacier, we gained the flanks of Gannett itself, although approaching clouds obscured the view. They warned us of the threat of storms, and theirs was no empty threat.

Our retreat was an epic, with every sort of weather (barring hurricanes and tornadoes) I'd ever heard of, climbing hardware humming and glowing an eerie blue with the St. Elmo's fire of approaching lightning.

I only partially remember that, as I was suffering from my first and only bout of altitude sickness. But I was hooked. I can remember the beauty of the approaching storm, seen from the top of the Titcomb Valley, and I remember thinking that it was literally the wildest place I'd ever seen, with no sign of man other than our footprints in the snow. Even before we'd made our hike out, I was already planning to return.

I had bought my own copy of *Wind River Trails* while in Wyoming, and used it to refresh my memories and create new plans over the coming winter. People I'd asked about Finis Mitchell had described him as up in years, an "old mountain man," and some were not even sure that he was still alive. But I found an address on the back cover of *Wind River Trails* and, on a whim, wrote the author a letter describing our trip of the previous summer, and asked if he still went into the mountains and whether he would consider going in with us.

Just over two weeks later, a letter arrived, written in a cramped, careful hand.

"If you went up Gannett from Big Sandy Openings in two and a half days, then you are a good man, and I would like to go up into the mountains with you," Finis Mitchell wrote me. "Call me, and we will set a date."

I knew only a little about Finis at the time: that he was widely recognized as the most knowledgeable individual alive when it came to the subject of the Wind River Range; that he had been a professional guide for years but was now in retirement; and that, in addition to being a backcountry expert and a guidebook author, he was also an accomplished photographer—virtually every postcard I'd seen during my first trip to the Winds carried Finis's photo credit.

We talked on the phone. He sounded as if he was up in years, which I expected. But he was ready to tackle any trail in the range that I was willing to try, and he not only refused my suggestion that I pay him—"I've been out of the guiding business for years"—he offered his home in Rock Springs as an overnight stop and staging area, and his stalwart Chevrolet Suburban as transportation over the sixty-odd miles of unpaved road that led to the trailhead.

Still, what I'd heard on the phone did not prepare me for what I saw when Chuck and Kay and I arrived in Rock Springs the following August. Chuck was a representative for several backcountry equipment manufacturers, and the three of us were done up in the latest gear—wind pants and anoraks, polypropylene undergarments, fleece jackets, ultralight backpacks and freestanding mountain tents, everything lightweight, high-tech, and the best that money could buy.

Finis, on the other hand, met us at the door of his home in blue-denim bib overalls and a cotton flannel shirt. He walked with a limp, supporting himself with one hand on the furniture as he went from room to room, and Emma, his wife, was always there to lend a hand when he needed steadying.

It gave us pause. But Emma's steady banter as she baked bread for our first days on the trail and expertly helped package foodstuffs for the backcountry (she had been Finis's cook during the years that he had guided) made it obvious that going into the mountains was something that Finis did often.

The next morning, before sunup, the Suburban was packed and we were ready to go. Chuck, Kay, and I were in our outdoor-shop finest, and Finis was wearing exactly what he'd had on the evening before—only now he'd added a feed-store cap and a thick-soled pair of hiking boots. He carried a staff in each hand as he got into the truck, and settled himself carefully into the driver's seat, as if doing it too fast would be painful.

Our trio exchanged looks. We didn't say a word, but we were thinking it—this might be a short trip. Saying good-bye to Emma, who told us, "Bring him back to me or tell me where you left him," we headed north, to the high country.

The moment he stepped out of the truck at the Green River Lakes trailhead, though, Finis was a changed man. He stood straighter, walked with a hint of bounce in his step, and was obviously raring to go. His outfit remained the ubiquitous bib overalls—during all the years I knew him, I never saw Finis wear anything else, not even to go out to dinner—but his backpack was the latest Jansport design, his tent the same, a small one-man bivouac model. He'd seemed pleased when Chuck and I had told him the day before that we would carry all of the food and cooking gear; he'd promptly taken his stove and billy pots out of his pack and filled up the empty space with additional camera equipment.

He carried no water with him on the trail, and advised us to do the same—"We'll have water straight from heaven everyplace I'm taking us." And he was in a hurry to leave the trailhead parking area behind. The view from the Green River Lakes trailhead was magnificent—a lake backdropped by a majestic table-peaked mountain, a vista of towering pines, and stone outcrops. But Finis assured us that this was just the "tourist view"—there would be better things to look at further on.

Following Finis in the backcountry was an experience in itself. He eschewed the use of established trails, calling them "main roads" and "over-traveled." Picking his way nimbly with a staff in each deerskin-gloved hand, he followed what he called "game trails," although we could not for the life of us distinguish a difference between the path we were supposedly following and the underbrush that surrounded it. Chuck and I shot compass readings whenever we could find an open spot in the trees, and tried our best to keep fixing our position on a topographic map. But after a while, we gave it up. The bearings always triangulated on blank areas. That first day, just when we figured that Finis had walked us in circles and truly lost us in the woods, we emerged from trees to the shores of a beautiful little lake fed by a tiny waterfall. And when Chuck and Kay and I scratched our heads and said that we were stumped, that we could not find the lake on our map, Finis simply replied, "Oh—*this* lake? No. I don't think it's on *any* map."

That was the way he was. He could walk through unmarked, untouched wilderness for hours, with no chart or compass, and lead us unerringly to small lakes, pristine streams, mountain-studded overlooks so beautiful that they made you want to weep at the splendor of it all. He wore thick glasses constantly, yet was always pointing out something—a dole sheep high on a snow-dappled ridge, an eagle nesting in a crag.

He took us to fish lakes that were well off the beaten path because "they needed it." Finis, we would discover, had stocked many of these lakes himself back during the Depression, when a layoff from his railroad job had turned him to guiding wealthy Eastern fishermen into the mountains. The Winds had contained hundreds of lakes at that time, but only five had contained trout. Finis put state-supplied trout fry into some 250 mountain lakes during the years that he was guiding—and every single fish was carried into the mountains in five-gallon milk cans, slung over the backs of pack horses. He felt stewardship for these lakes that he had stocked, and he asked us to fish the over-populated ones to help balance out the natural food chain.

Even the animals of the mountains seemed to have special kinship with him. He told us how, when a summer snowstorm caught him on an exposed ridge, he had found a group of dole sheep and followed them through the whiteout to a hollow where, for two days, Finis and the sheep had holed up together and waited out the storm. On another occasion, when he'd gotten wind that a group of illegal hunters was coming in to poach elk in a remote region of the range, Finis had hiked in ahead of them and driven the herd over a ridge and into a valley several miles away from where the poachers would be operating.

His limp, he told us, was from a broken hip that had never healed right. He'd gotten it falling into a crevasse during an extended solo backpacking trip when he was already well into his seventies. He'd climbed out of the crevasse, unassisted, and then made his way to the trail-head, eighteen miles away, on his hands and knees. He'd pulled his backpack behind him on a length of climbing rope because, "It was a new pack, and a good one, and I didn't want to leave it."

And even that trip was one Finis remembered fondly. He'd made it, he told us, because the U.S. Geological Survey maps of the area had the Continental Divide running in the wrong place and, when he'd called the USGS to tell them, they'd said that they did not have the resources to resurvey it. So Finis had done it himself and sent them the data.

"They changed the maps and made 'em right," he reported happily.

Finis was eighty-two years old the summer I first met him, but that did not stop us from having a long friendship and sharing many happy trips into his mountains.

He did slow down a little as time went on. For years, doctors had advised him to consider corrective surgery for his old hip fracture, but the recovery period would be lengthy, and he had never wanted to spend up to a year away from the familiar surroundings of his beloved mountains. So he had adjusted by lightening his pack.

Finis left his tent at home and took to camping rough, sleeping on the ground, using only a waterproof tarp as a shelter and carried only the tiniest of cookstoves with a single pot and a pan that doubled as a plate. A minimal selection of clothes, a pair of sticks to steady himself on the trail, and he was ready to travel.

I always carried a tent large enough for the two of us when we traveled, but he refused to use it.

"I'm old," he told me. "I get up too often during the night; I'd keep you up."

But I knew the truth was that, if Finis did not carry the tent in himself, he did not want to sleep in it. He enjoyed his self-sufficiency.

One time, as we camped on a plateau high above a beautiful mountain-ringed lake, after I had put up the tent and

Finis had decided once again not to use it, I announced that I, too, would sleep rough under the stars that night. Eyes atwinkle, Finis had shown me how he rigged his bedroll—he found a spot with a slight grade to it, laid down his rubberized nylon tarp, and put his sleeping pad and mummy bag on the downhill side. Then he put two turns of the uphill edge of the tarp around one of his ubiquitous hiking staves, so he could pull cover over himself if it rained during the night; the water would run off the top, and drain down the hill.

I did just as he said, but we had no sooner bedded down that evening than I found myself migrating down the slight slope on which I was sleeping. Every time I tossed or turned, I would roll off the ground-pad and off the tarp, onto the sod. Finis, meantime, was snoring peacefully not ten feet away, staying on his pad like a ship firmly aground in the shallows.

I found my parka and wind pants, rolled them up, and stuffed them under the downhill side of my bag to wedge myself in place. This seemed to work. Then I heard the first peals of thunder rolling up the valley—a full-fledged storm was headed our way.

A storm in the city, or even one in farmland, cannot hold a candle to a storm in the mountains. In the mountains, the cliffs and valleys echo and reverberate with the sound of a thunderstorm's fury; exploding artillery shells could not have a more immediate presence.

Even allowing for this natural amplification, I could tell that the storm headed our way was a doozy, but Finis slept on, his snoring increasing a bit as if to keep up over the racket of the thunder. Lightning lit up the valley around us in stark, blue-white relief, and I could see the treetops whipping around the lakeside below us. But still Finis slept. So, when the first fat raindrops fell, I pulled the tarp over myself, heard Finis do the same, and instantly was encapsulated beneath the dark and waterproof sheet.

It was miserable. The tarp kept the rain out—at first—but it also trapped in the heat and moisture rising from my body. It was like trying to sleep in a steam bath, and a noisy steam bath, at that. The heavy, pelting rain kept a constant tempo on the outside of the tarp, like a thousand manic drummers beating tempos on my body. No one could sleep in conditions such as this; I was sure of it. But I knew that I would be instantly soaked it I tried to lift the tarp off for relief.

A few minutes later, the rain was accompanied by a howling wind that seemed determined to rip the tarp away, and I was certain that parts of it were flapping up from time to time, letting in portions of the deluge.

Finally, when I felt cold rainwater dribbling down the back of my neck, the lure of the tight, dry tent became irresistible. Tossing off the tarp, I gathered the mummy bag and ground-pad and sprinted barefoot through the torrents and the mud, barely taking the time to unzip the fly before launching myself into the dry confines within.

Even so, my short sprint through the storm had thoroughly wetted the bag and ground-pad, as well as soaking me through to the skin. I climbed into the sopping nylon and shivered through the night, trying to stay warm.

And in the morning, Finis was dry, and, when I remarked on the fury of the previous evening's storm, he had replied, in all earnestness, "Oh? Did it rain?"

He may have camped light as the years went on, but the one area where Finis did not stint was his camera equipment. His Pentax, a selection of lenses, a tripod, and an ample supply of film went wherever he went. Packing the camera and lenses meant that he would not be able to carry his fishing gear, but he and I had worked out an arrangement long before—he would photograph me while I fished, and then, after a while, he would take the fly rod while I shot pictures of him with my camera. It made the trips into the mountains even more special, sharing the rod and watching, through the camera viewfinder, the beauty of a man at peace with a place he knew well, perfectly at home in surroundings that most would call a howling wilderness.

Finis was a Christian, and he thought of his trips to the mountains as prayer, an extended communion with his Maker in country that had been left as God had created it. He often left the campsite to pray alone, and he carried a Bible that he read during our daylight rest stops. When we talked in the evening, under the starlight, it was usually of his thankfulness that Jesus had died for his sins and of the eagerness that he had to meet, face-to-face, the master Artist who had sculpted the Wind River Range.

Still, Finis had his blue periods, as well. Sometimes, as we looked across a magnificent valley, ringed by snow-capped mountains and divided by a solitary river, tears would well up in his eyes, and he would say, "This could be the last time I come here. I may never see this place again."

"But, Finis," I would tell him. "You're seeing it now."

And he would agree and be grateful, and things would be better for a time.

On one trip in, when Chuck and Kay were with us, Finis's hip had troubled him more than ever, and Chuck and I had lightened his pack at each rest stop so he could go on. That night, he had been silent as we pitched the tents, and Chuck and Kay, after a hasty conference, had surveyed the food bags, dug a small pit, and used our billy pans to create a modest Dutch oven in which they baked, with wood coals above and below it, a simple cake. Kay made a frosting with eggs, butter, and sugar, and we topped the creation off with a candle from one of our lanterns before marching up to where Finis sat, lost in thought. Lighting the candle, we launched into a boisterous, if off-key, rendition of "Happy Birthday to You," and he grinned broadly but stopped us.

180

"It's not my birthday," Finis said. And we knew that. Finis had told us on his first trip in with us that he had been born in the winter of 1900. He'd written the date in our guidebooks and told us to keep his hundredth birthday open on our calendars, as he planned a big celebration in the mountains and wanted us all to be there.

But Chuck only nodded and asked, "Finis, how old is the Wind River Range?"

"Oh, scientists say eighty million years," Finis said, adding, as he always did, "God made it Himself on the day of creation, eighty million years ago."

Chuck nodded again, and added, ". . . *today!*"

And as Kay led us in singing "Happy Birthday" again, Finis chuckled—he was the only person I ever knew that literally went "hee, hee, hee" as he laughed—and repeated, "Eighty million years ago today!"

Finis could be coaxed out of his doldrums, but age kept taking its toll. On our last trip into the mountains, I hired a horsepacker to take us in, but it turned out that sitting in a saddle was even more painful on Finis's hip than walking. When I saw that he was in agony, I called a rest, got our rucksacks out of the equipment panniers and then, marking our campsite on the map for the horsepacker, set off with Finis on foot (on mountain trails, a person on foot can almost always travel more swiftly than a string of packhorses).

When we got to the lake where we intended to camp, Finis sat on a rock and rested while I got water boiling for cocoa, setting out some light provisions to snack on while we waited for the pack string. He was gazing up into the distance, and I knew what he was looking at.

Just above a ridge, Finis could see the snowy top of a mountain—Mitchell Peak.

There is a government policy against naming landmasses after living Americans, but the government had made an exception with Mitchell Peak. It had literally taken an act of Congress, but, in recognition of his stewardship of the Wind River Range, the Geological Survey had asked Finis to pick out his favorite mountain, and they'd named it for him—a perpetual natural monument to a man who loved nature above everything except God.

"How many times have you been up there?" I asked him, breaking the silence.

"Oh . . . dozens and dozens," he said softly. "The view from up there on Mitchell, it's just—"

And then he fell silent for a time, and he looked back up at me, eyes damp through his thick glasses.

"Will you take me there?" Finis asked. "Will you take me up Mitchell Peak?"

I looked back at him, wondering.

"This trip?" I asked. I knew his hip was troubling him.

"No," he told me sadly. "Not this trip. I'd never make it. But if I can just get this hip better. Maybe I'll have that surgery so I can do it. But . . . if I get to where I can make the climb, will you go with me, Tom? Will you take me up there, so I can stand on top of Mitchell Peak one last time?"

I thought for a moment. The climb up Mitchell Peak is not technical; but there are steep places. I doubted that a man in his eighties, even a healthy one without a badly healed hip fracture, could make it. But he obviously wanted it very, very much. I nodded.

"I promise," I told him. "I'll take you up Mitchell Peak."

I made that promise with good intentions. We corresponded over following months about ways that we could climb Mitchell Peak. Finis had friends in the Forest Service; if I could get hold of a four-wheel-drive vehicle, he thought that he could get permission for us to drive up a fire-trail that would put us within a day-hike of the summit. But Finis was still talking with his doctors, weighing the surgery, and I had started working with a new publishing company that was taking up almost all of my time. We discussed some dates that would not work for me, and then we put the trip off; first once and then twice. It was always something I planned to get to, but never something I did.

And then it was too late.

Finis's letters stopped coming. There wasn't the card at Christmas. I made some inquiries with mutual friends and learned that Finis was with us no longer. He was sitting at the feet of the Artist who had made his Wind River Range.

I have never been to the summit of Mitchell Peak. I intend to do it, someday. I would like to see the view that my old friend so enjoyed and to take out a Bible and read it there alone, surrounded by another great work of the Master.

But I will not stand on that summit without my own pang of regret. I had, after all, made a promise. And even though there were reasons—conflicts, circumstances, dates put off with good intentions—the fact remains that I waited too long. I'd made a promise, and I did not keep it.

True, to Finis, it undoubtedly no longer matters. He is now in a glory that vastly overshadows any earthly mountain vista. He is happy and talking daily with the One he loves more than anything.

But it matters to me. And I imagine that it will until the day that I die.

I cannot think of my old friend, Finis Mitchell, without remembering his grace and his dignity and the reverent and deep, abiding love he had for God and His wilderness. If I close my eyes I can still picture him, clad in his plaid shirt and "overhauls," a

feed cap perched on his weathered, white head, pointing out some marvel that he wanted to share, almost always some marvel that required him to point high into the sky, because, with Finis, it seemed that his eyes were always lifted up to heaven.

But I cannot remember my wonderful old friend without a tinge of regret, either. I do not know, after all, if he ever made that one, last trip that he'd always wanted to make to the top of Mitchell Peak. But I certainly know that I did not take him there.

Eventually, I know, I will get over that unfulfilled promise— it may not happen in this life, but I know that it will in the next. Because I know without a doubt that I will see my friend Finis again.

Perhaps we will scale the heights of heaven together. But when that happens, he will not be needing my help, because I have it on the authority of the Bible, in 1 Corinthians 15:52–53, that age and decay will have no presence there, and Finis will be able to roam and climb forever, because Finis will stay forever young.

That, then, is the kind of regret I know I will get over. I put off our appointment too many times, but I know my old friend will forgive me. But what if I had put off something of a much more crucial nature?

Just ten years ago as I write this, I made a friend on the island of Great Exuma in the Bahamas, a wonderful, vibrant and intelligent man named Ed Haxby. Ed was trained as a marine biologist, and he had gone to the Bahamas soon after graduating from college. He worked for the Morton Salt Company on the island of Great Inagua, where he introduced the process of aquaculture (raising edible crabs) in their salt ponds—a process that improved the quality of the salt derived from the ponds, produced a byproduct (crabmeat) that added an additional revenue stream, and worked so well that it is now used virtually everywhere in the world that sea salt is derived from ocean water.

While on Great Inagua, Ed fell in love with and married a local girl. In time, they had two children, a boy, and then a girl. And Ed, a loving and caring father, was concerned over how they

184

would be educated, as Great Inagua was a very sparsely popu-
lated island, with little in the way of schools.

Ed told me how he discussed the situation with his company
and how they offered to transfer him back to the United States,
to company headquarters in Chicago, where his children could
have access to some of the best schools in the world, from grade
school all the way to university.

"I appreciated that offer," Ed later told me. "But I also knew
that I could never accept it. Except for short visits for medical care
in Miami, my wife had never been away from Great Inagua, and
I was certain that she would die if I were to remove her and take
her to a big city in a cold climate."

So Ed took stock of his resources. He was a trained biologist
and a highly accomplished scuba diver, having spent thousands
of hours underwater in his studies. He knew the sea life of the
Bahamas as well as any man alive, and he was a garrulous individual who enjoyed the company of others.

Ed made some phone calls and a few flights to others of the Bahamas Out Islands, and he discovered that the school system on
Great Exuma had a wonderful new headmaster who'd received
very high marks from those in the educational know.

With an airstrip capable of handling commercial traffic from
the United States, Great Exuma was more populated than Great
Inagua but still far from spoiled, with much of the land still in
its natural state. It was, Ed judged, a place where his wife and
his family could thrive, and there was a business available—a
boat livery and outboard motor dealership, with a dive shop and
charter business attached. The price was right and, with savings
accrued over years of living frugally on Great Inagua, Ed bought
it and moved his family north to Great Exuma.

I met Ed the first year he had his business there. He had just
finished a weeklong course at a professional dive school in Florida,
where he had earned a divemaster's certificate. With that, he was
qualified to run dive charters, and he delighted in showing me
the waters around his new island home, from the tongue-and-

185

*groove coral reef formations that covered the great Exuma Shoals,
to the mysterious blue holes—the entries to cave systems that in-
haled and exhaled seawater in rhythm with the tides.*

*In time, Ed returned to Florida and got the necessary train-
ing to pass his exam as a scuba instructor. He hired staff to run
his outboard motor business, and trained young local men to
work as mates and divemasters on his charter boats. He was one
of the first people in the Bahamas to promote diving as "eco-
tourism," and he did it better than anyone else I ever met there.
I remember making dives with Ed in which we never moved
more than twenty feet along the reef—yet he had shown me literally hundreds of undersea life forms by the time we returned
to the surface.*

*I returned and dived with Ed several times. He never charged
me a cent—at first because I was a writer, doing stories for dive
magazines; and later because we were friends, and we could ex-
plore new dive sites together. In between trips, we would talk on
the phone, or see one another at diving industry conventions, and
he was always inviting me down to Great Exuma, offering his
porch, or the cuddy of a friend's sailboat, for lodging if I could not
scare up a magazine story to provide a hotel room.*

*Then one year, in January, I missed Ed at DEMA, the diving
industry's biggest annual convention. We almost always had been
able to either find each other, either on the convention floor, or
through the directories at the convention hotels. So when I got
home, I called him.*

*He hadn't, he said, attended DEMA that year. He'd been in
the hospital.*

*"This winter, one of the clients on my boat was an oncologist,
and I showed him something I'd noticed, a lump about the size
of a golf ball that had appeared under my arm," he said. "He
told me that I'd better get it checked out in a clinical setting, so,
two weeks later, when I was scheduled to be in Miami to finalize
the order on a new dive boat, I made an appointment with a doc-
tor my client had recommended.*

"He told me that he suspected I had lymphatic cancer—a fairly advanced stage of it. I canceled the order for my boat and checked into the hospital. My surgeons confirmed the diagnosis, removed quite a few of my lymph nodes, and gave me radiation therapy."

There being little in the way of sophisticated medical treatment on Great Exuma, the doctors had sent Ed home with everything he needed to do his own chemotherapy. Ed's wife had been giving him chemo on the porch of their island home two times a week. The prognosis was uncertain.

I went silent on the phone. In all the times I had dived and visited with Ed, I had never spoken with him about eternity, never talked with him about Jesus Christ and God's plan for salvation. It had always been reefs and ocean and fish, divers we knew and places we'd been.

Suddenly none of that seemed the least bit important. I knew I had a question to ask my friend. But it seemed so hard to do it over the phone, and I didn't want to discourage him with talk of dying when he was so obviously fighting, and fighting hard, for his life.

I took a deep breath.

"Are you diving?" I asked him.

He wasn't, he told me. His last dive had been with his clients, two days before he'd left to go see the doctors in Miami. That was the hardest part, he said. His friends had been supportive, and his family was closer than ever, but he'd never thought that he might lose diving, and then, suddenly, he'd had it snatched away.

Snatched away. Here was another opportunity to present the gospel story, but still, I was squeamish.

"Who's running your charter?" I asked him.

"My divemaster," he said. "He's off for a couple of weeks this summer, though. I'll probably have to hire another one to bridge the gap."

"Don't," I told him impulsively. I had a valid divemaster's certificate; it wouldn't cost much to activate my insurance for Caribbean work. "I'm coming down to help you. I know the sites you dive; I've run your boats. I won't cost you a cent, and people would probably get a kick out of diving with somebody whose work they've read in the dive magazines."

Now Ed was silent.

"Tom," he began. "We'd love to see you. But you don't have to work—just come on down—"

"Nonsense," I cut him off. "You need a divemaster; I am a divemaster. It's a done deal."

And the next call I made was to American Airlines, booking myself on a flight to Fort Lauderdale, and from there, to Georgetown, Great Exuma. We'd have plenty of time together when we got there. Plenty of time to talk.

My gear was packed and my schedule was getting clear when Ed called me back, about two weeks before I was supposed to go to the islands.

"Don't come down," he told me. His cancer was relapsing, and the doctors were putting him back in the hospital. He wouldn't be on the island and, besides, he'd had some charters cancel, so he was pulling his boats out of the water and having them overhauled while he was gone.

I wanted to ask him a question again, but he seemed so down. We made an arrangement—we'd talk in a month. I'd call him; the therapy was tiring him, and he was having a hard time remembering appointments.

A month later, when I got Ed on the phone, it was obvious that the news from the hospital had not been good. Regardless of what happened, Ed told me, the doctors had said that he would never be able to dive again. He was selling his businesses, making certain his family was secure, tidying things up.

"Ed," I asked him straight out. "Are you dying?"

"Yes," he told me. His voice was very straightforward, very matter-of-fact. "It might be weeks, might be months. But they're pretty sure I won't make it to Christmas."

I took a deep breath. I'd so wanted to have this conversation face-to-face. But, obviously, it was now or never.

"Listen, Ed," I finally said. "Doctors can be wrong, and I hope yours are. I hope that we not only visit again, I hope we'll be diving together again for years to come."

"I don't think that we will," he muttered.

"If that's the case," I asked him, "can you tell me something? Whenever it happens, whether it's next week or fifty years from now, are you certain—absolutely certain—that you'll be going to heaven when you die?"

The phone went silent, and I realized Ed was weeping.

"Oh, Tom," he said in a quiet voice. "You are such a good, good friend."

I gave him a moment, and then he continued.

"For the last couple of months, people have been talking to me," he said, getting his voice back. "They've talked with me about alternative therapies, setting up the finances for my family, ways of taking care of things. But you're—"

His voice broke again.

"You're the only one," he continued, "that has asked me the one thing that really truly matters. Yes, Tom. I'm going to heaven. I'm certain of it."

And then, getting strength back into his voice, he told me how he had accepted Jesus Christ into his life as his personal Savior, years before; how he had, in recent months, spoken at great length with every single member of his family and made certain that they knew Christ as their Savior as well.

And that difficult phone call became a time of rejoicing.

"Behold," says the Bible in 2 Corinthians 6:2, "now is the accepted time; behold, now is the day of salvation."

When He sent His disciples out to carry His message, Jesus Christ wanted to reach as many people as possible. He felt this mission to be so critical that He wanted His disciples to concentrate upon it entirely and not even to be concerned with matters pertaining to their own subsistence.

"And he called unto him the twelve, and began to send them forth by two and two; and gave them power over unclean spirits;

and commanded them that they should take nothing for their journey, save a staff only; no scrip, no bread, no money in their purse," records Mark 6:7–8.

Jesus asked His disciples to concentrate, not on their journey, but on His mission. The Jews of ancient times did not require their priests and religious officials to do secular work; instead, each member of the other eleven tribes of Israel gave a tenth of what he earned to the tribe of Levi—the tribe dedicated to serving God— and so supported the priesthood. Knowing this, Jesus asked His disciples to have faith that they, too, would be supported by the people they met as they traveled. Plainly, the gospel message was so important to Jesus Christ that He wanted nothing to supercede it, nothing to get in the way of the good news of redemption being spread. A disciple stopping to buy food for himself, or a disciple eating his own provisions, and not dining in the company of others, was a disciple who was not witnessing. And a disciple who put off witnessing was a disciple who took the chance of missing people with Christ's message, and risking the possibility that they would perish in hell without knowing that salvation was right there, literally within their grasp.

I know what it's like to procrastinate. I know what it's like to put things off. With my friend Finis, I put our last trip off so long that it never took place, and I regret that deeply. But I am so very, extremely, eternally happy that I had that conversation with my friend Ed. I am so glad I made certain that he knew how heaven was gained.

Ed and I never spoke again. He passed away a few months later. And I was sad for his family, and I mourned for myself. But I did not feel sorry for Ed. He had gone to a place so beautiful that the reefs and depths of the Caribbean must seem shabby in comparison.

I'm glad Ed and I spoke, because four of the saddest words in the English language are "I waited too long."

If you are a Christian . . . if you know Jesus Christ as your Savior . . . and if you have someone who's important to you, someone you care for, someone you love, the most important thing you can possibly do is make certain that they know how they can receive Christ as their Savior, as well. The alternative is too horrible to contemplate; the remedy too simple to ignore. I know it can seem difficult to bring the subject up. With Ed, I certainly took months.

But I'm so glad that I didn't wait too long. I'm so glad I know where he is.

Jesus already did the really difficult part of seeing us to heaven. All we have to do is go and tell.

Do you have a friend? A family member? Someone you love?
How are you going to show them that you care about them?
A witness delayed can be a witness undelivered.
How long are you willing to wait?

9

THE LEGACY

For thou shalt be his witness unto all men
of what thou hast seen and heard.

ACTS 22:15

It has been my good fortune, over the years, to become proficient at a number of interesting things. I have bicycled long distances, climbed and skied and angled, been rated as an expert in karate, and become a good shot with both a rifle and a pistol and a fair contender at trap and skeet. And in all of those endeavors I have, at some point or another, taught someone else how to do it.

As a graduate student at the University of Toledo, I taught cross-country skiing for both the city parks-and-recreation department and a local outdoors store. I taught rock-climbing with the university's Recreation and Leisure Education department, helped others learn to become long-distance cyclists, and trained aspiring *karate-ka* in my position as *sempei* (senior student) at my sensei's karate-dojo.

While a writer at the Campbell-Ewald advertising agency, I taught my division's president to fly-cast. We would walk across the street to the lake in front of the Chevrolet Engineering headquarters and cast onto its still waters at lunch time, usually drawing a crowd, which waited to see if we would catch a fish, which, of course, we did not, as the lake was ornamental and there were no fish there.

But when it came to scuba diving, I drew the line. I enjoyed it . . . a lot. I did not enjoy diving with novice divers—they were clumsy, they could not keep themselves in trim, they churned up the sediment on the bottom, and they ran into one another. The noise of them overbreathing their regulators frightened away the sealife, and whenever I dived with beginners, it seemed that they got themselves into predicaments that I had to get them out of. I thought of neophyte divers in the same way I thought of large dogs: They were usually friendly but generally clumsy, as well, and they often seemed to leave their common sense on the boat, requiring me to watch them and have common sense enough for both of us.

Nor was I alone in this opinion. During one trip to North Carolina, I was chatting with George Purifoy, the owner of Olympus Dive Center—one of the East Coast's most famous—when I was amazed to learn that he, who ran a dive-training-agency-recognized shop, was not a scuba instructor.

"I'll never be," he told me. "I love diving. It's my hobby. If I have to start teaching people to dive, I won't love it anymore. It will become a job. So I refuse to become a scuba instructor. I hire scuba instructors and put them to work for me."

A wise man, I thought at the time. And that was my attitude for years—let someone else take the training and do the teaching. I knew enough to do my own diving, and I was happy at it.

Still, times came up when an instructor's certification would have been handy. I remember having lunch with a minister of tourism on a small Caribbean island—a minister of tourism who was considering destroying several world-renowned reefs and dive sites to put in moorings for the cruise-ship industry.

Of course, I was opposed to this, and I argued my case with facts and figures—the amount of per-capita on-island spending by the typical dive tourist as opposed to the typical cruise-ship passenger, the tendency of cruise-ship ports to attract pickpockets and flimflam artists, and the fact that cruise-ship moorings were nothing but the underwater version of paving paradise.

I'd like to think I was successful at this (the moorings never went in), but what I really had wanted to do at the time was put a scuba tank on the fellow, take him underwater, and show him what was at risk. As a scuba instructor, I could have done this, but as a private diver, I would be neither prudent nor insured.

Things such as this were on my mind when *Scuba Times* magazine called and asked me to take a course and do a story on what was involved to become a scuba instructor. The magazine was willing to arrange the course fees, so it wouldn't cost me a penny; I would, in fact, be paid to take a course that would run others upwards of four figures out of their own pockets.

It was too good a deal to pass up. Still resolved that I would never teach anyone to dive, I took them up on it, and called a local shop—Divers Incorporated in Ann Arbor, Michigan—to enroll in their upcoming Instructor Development Course.

Divers Incorporated was owned at the time by Richard Roost, a brawny man with a walrus moustache and a mop of dark, sandy hair, a fellow who always seemed to be on the hint of a smile and had that rarest of conversational talents—the ability to listen thoughtfully for minutes on end. He was one of the Great Lakes' most respected deep wreck divers and had visited shipwrecks at depths un-dreamed-of by most divers, yet he would listen to a newer diver's description of their trip to a popular dive resort as if he were hearing about the eighth wonder of the world. And the best part was, he wasn't faking it. He didn't see any hierarchy—didn't think of the diving he did as in any way superior to the novice's swim on a regularly visited reef. He simply thought of them as different, and that at-titude, more than anything, made Divers Incorporated one of the busiest dive shops in the Midwest.

When I signed up for the course, I lacked a single pre-requisite—the Medic First Aid rating that would show me as proficient in both basic first aid and oxygen adminis-tration. So Richard took it upon himself to certify me, patiently explaining everything, making certain that ev-erything was clear before moving on, being a model teacher—which, indeed, he was.

During breaks, we chatted, compared notes on dives we'd both enjoyed, and shared a few meals together. Even before the formal Instructor Development Course began, we were already becoming friends.

A large box arrived from the Professional Association of Diving Instructors, packed with books on agency stan-dards, course outlines, manuals, legal and marketing hand-books, samples of a seemingly endless variety of forms, vi-sual aids, and waterproof underwater lesson-plan slates. When I asked Richard which of these I should read, he looked at me blankly and replied, "Well—all of it." So I set to it and got to the first day of class brimming with facts, figures, and precedents.

The IDC, as it was called, was an intense, six-day-long course that required us to arrive at the shop at 8:00 in the morning, do our classwork from then until 5:00 or 6:00, with a one-hour break for lunch in between, and then go home and study until 10:00 or so to be ready for the next day. Richard explained the first morning that we would be learning nothing new about diving. All eight students—people drawn from all over the Midwest—were proficient and even expert at scuba. We were, instead, going to be taught to teach. But he warned us not to be lax about this.

We knew the reason for the warning. The IDC is one of the few courses in scuba diving in which the person doing the teaching—the Course Director, in this case, Richard—is not the person doing the certifying. That would take place on the weekend following the course, during the IE, or Instructor Exam, which would be conducted by an examiner dispatched from PADI headquarters, in California. We had to pass the IDC to take the IE, but other than that, it counted for nothing. How we did in class did not matter. Relationships formed with the course staff did not matter. We would be tested by a stranger who, while fair, would fail us without a second thought if we did not measure up, and people failed the PADI exam regularly.

"I have never had a student pass my IDC and fail the IE," Richard told us on the first morning of class. "But that's because of dedication. I want you to put your life on hold and concentrate entirely on your coursework over the next week. If you can't do that, you won't pass, and you'll ruin my record. If you can't make that commitment, it's better to pull out now and wait for the next course—it'll be less trying for each of us."

He looked around. All eight heads nodded. We were in for the duration.

We saw two complementary sides of Richard over the next six days. Our written exams were mostly multiple choice, so there was little subjectivity involved in grading them. But on our teaching demonstrations, done in the classroom and in the pool, this naturally kind man was

197

ruthless, pointing out minor flaws, constantly urging us to reach down and find something better. When teaching in the pool, we acted as "students" for one another, and Richard would take us aside and have us fake "mistakes" for our peers, little slip-ups that would be easy to overlook. Those who missed these were made to do their teaching exercises over again.

But we didn't think of him as an ogre; we knew that he was deliberately being tougher on us than the examiner would be in the IE. And proof of this came in the fact that he was available to us twenty-four hours a day. If we found something unclear in our reading at three in the morning, he told us, we were told to call him for clarification. Three times, I found references to materials I did not have, and Richard loaned them to me, once, he came into the shop an hour early so I could view one particular instructional videotape before class began.

Toward the end of the class, we were doing open-water evaluations at a local lake, and I remember him hovering close over the shoulder of each instructor candidate, watching for even the slightest flaw in technique, staying near so nothing would be missed in the diminished visibility of the lake.

Midway through the course, we took a break just after I'd given a demonstration. Richard told me, "That was good, Tom. I can tell you've spoken to groups before; you're going to make a great instructor. Your students will do well."

"Thanks," I replied. "But I don't really plan on having students."

He paused and stood there as the others filed out around us.

"I hope you'll reconsider that," he told me. "What you have here is a gift, and gifts are given for a purpose, you know. You're supposed to use them."

And with that, he joined the others and filed upstairs.

At the end of our course, Richard made an announcement.

"Every night," he said, "I've been telling you to go home and study. Tonight's the exception. Tomorrow the IE begins. Go out this evening, take a walk, take your spouse to dinner if you have them with you, and get to bed early. Get relaxed and get rested; that's the best way to be ready for tomorrow."

It was good advice but hard to take. I know that I resisted the urge to crack the books, but I was still lying awake, long after midnight. I'd put a lot of hours into taking this course, and passing the exam was important to me.

"But why?" a small voice nagged at me from my subconscious. "You don't ever intend to teach this. You don't ever intend to have students. Why are you worried? If you don't pass, what does it matter?"

The next morning, ten people—eight from our IDC, and two who had taken their course out of state—were at a local hotel and convention center, ready to begin their exams. I arrived in a freshly pressed sport coat and tie—highly unusual plumage for me—and I was amused to see that most of my classmates had, as well. Richard had mentioned that formal business attire was once mandatory for IEs and was still not a bad idea.

Chatting, having coffee before we started, I learned that one of the out-of-staters had taken the exam before and failed. And the part he had failed on was a closed-book examination on PADI's general standards and procedures—the first test we'd take that morning. That would be followed by quizzes in physiology, marine biology, general diving knowledge, equipment, and planning dives with PADI's two forms of recreational dive planners—the well-known PADI dive tables, and the less-used Wheel®, a simple mechanical computer. We could fail up to two of these quizzes and retake them later in the weekend, but the general standards-and-procedures test was a one-shot deal. If we failed it, we were welcome to take the rest of the exam, but we would not pass.

We sat down and listened as Brad Ware, the examiner, briefed us on what we would do that day. He did his best to put us at ease, but that only seemed to accentuate the tension. Had someone popped a balloon about then, I'm pretty sure all ten of us would have keeled over from heart attacks.

And then we began.

I have a technique for taking examinations. One quickly answers all the questions one can on a quick pass through, and then one goes back and reviews the questions that weren't immediately clear. About ninety of the test's one hundred questions fell into that former category, so I was immediately set at ease—even in the unlikely event that I was wrong in 10 percent of the questions I'd answered so far, I would still have done well enough to pass.

I went back through the other ten, figured most of them out, took an educated guess at a couple, and was left with a single question. I read it again, read it a fourth, fifth and sixth time. Then I saw what the problem was. I raised my hand.

Brad came over and hunkered down next to my chair.

"What's up?" he asked.

"This question," I whispered. "None of the possible answers are correct."

He smiled. He'd been an examiner for quite a while, but obviously he hadn't heard this one before.

"Why do you say that?" Brad asked, patronizing me.

"PADI changed a number of standards on January first of this year," I explained, "and one of the courses affected was the one that this question concerns. The standard was changed—it still appears in the old form in the manual, but the correction was issued in the Training Bulletin. I know, because I copied the new information from the training information into my manual."

"Let me see that."

Brad read the question from my exam book and nodded.

"Pretend this was December thirty-first of last year," he said. "Would the question have an answer then?"

I nodded.

"Then use that as your answer," Brad told me.

Richard, while not an evaluator for the exam, had come along to help Brad as a proctor. He was standing against a near wall and had heard the entire exchange.

When I looked up, I saw that he was grinning.

I finished the standards course, exchanged it for a stack of quizzes, and finished those. One called for the use of a calculator and both forms of the dive planner, but still, I was done more than an hour early. I could have gone over everything a third time, but figured that a long lunch break would do me more good than agonizing over my answers. I turned them in to Brad, who whispered, "You've passed general standards and procedures—congratulations."

Then he graded what I'd given him, and he shook my hand.

"You've passed these, too," he said. "See you at the pool."

The pool work was anticlimactic, as the water was where all of the candidates were most comfortable—most of us dived at least weekly, twelve months a year. The twelve-hundred-yard swim exam was actually relaxing, and we joked and bantered as we did our exercises.

But as we were changing to go back to the hotel for our classroom demonstrations, I learned that two of the candidates—one from our IDC, and one of the out-of-staters—had each failed one of the quizzes. They would retake them in the morning, before we did our dives at the local lake.

The classroom work was fun, if trying. I did a session on emergency decompression and opened it by taking out a metal wastebasket stuffed with paper, a fire extinguisher, and a match.

"Knowing what to do in an emergency and having an emergency on purpose are two different things," I said. "For instance, I have here a fire extinguisher. That being the case," I continued, putting the wastebasket on Brad's desk where his briefcase sat, "does anyone mind if I go ahead and set this on fire?"

Brad looked at me, grinning, and I proceeded to explain that recreational divers learn some things that they are not expected to incorporate into their plans—that they were there for emergency only.

When I finished, Brad smiled, saying, "You're going to be a good teacher."

But his score wasn't perfect, so I asked, "If I'd set the wastebasket on fire, would you have given me a hundred?"

"We'll never know, will we?" Brad chuckled.

But I was still mulling over his comment—*you're going to be a good teacher.*

I wasn't.

Was I?

That echoed the next morning as I pulled into the parking lot at the lake. My classmate who'd failed a quiz was there, puzzling over the PADI Wheel® dive planner.

"This is what got me yesterday," he said sadly. Like most people, he had done almost all of his planning work with tables. "I don't know if I'm going to pass this."

"Sure you are," I told him. "This thing isn't that hard to figure. Grab a seat."

And with that, I took him to a nearby picnic table and ran through example after example until I was sure he'd caught on.

"Thanks," he said. He shook my hand, his gratitude obvious, before walking away.

"I thought you weren't planning on becoming a teacher," said a voice behind me.

I turned. It was Richard.

"I'm not," I said.

"I don't know," Richard returned, nodding at the back of my newly relieved classmate. "It looks to me as if you already are."

The lake sessions went as smoothly as the pool sessions. The one moment of comic relief came when I was kneeling on the dive platform in a mist of silt raised by our activities. My assignment had been to evaluate how my "class" cleared their dive masks, and as I lined them up, I noticed that one diver was hovering off to the side.

Aha, I thought to myself. *Brad told somebody to pretend to float away, to see if I'd notice they were missing.*

Clanking on my tank with my dive knife, I got the diver's attention and pantomimed forcefully that he should take his place on the platform.

He did. It was Brad.

I'd mistaken my examiner for one of the "students."

But I passed, as did all of my classmates, including the one who'd had to retake the quiz. One of the out-of-staters failed, but it was hard to feel sorry for him; three of us had offered to work with him on his weak subject, and he had brushed us off, saying, "I can take care of myself."

As for Richard, he was delighted—and you could tell that it was not simply because his 100-percent pass rate was still intact.

I saw Richard often over the next couple of weeks. He didn't nag at me about teaching; that wasn't his style. Richard had said his piece once, and now that decision was entirely up to me.

Mostly, we talked about wreck diving. Richard was about to take off on a trip to the East Coast to dive on the *Andrea Doria,* a wreck he'd dreamed of for years. He and I spoke about going up to Lake Superior together when he got back. We had a roster of wrecks we wanted to visit together. Some of the folks from my IDC had also talked to Richard about a course in teaching the wreck diving specialty. He asked if I was interested.

"Possibly," I told him. I didn't want to reopen the subject of teaching. "Have a good trip to the *Doria*. Take lots of pictures, and I'll see you when you get back."

But I never did see Richard alive again. One week later, one of my IDC classmates called with bad news. Richard had gone missing on his *Doria* dive. Other divers had gone in looking for him the next day and found his lifeless body floating in the ship's ballroom, with no sign of a struggle or panic. As one of the divers told the authorities: "He looked as if he had fallen asleep."

That assessment was eerily accurate. Both of the tanks on Richard's back had been empty, although the two spare cylinders clipped to his harness were still full and untouched; he had drowned without even attempting to go to his back-up cylinders. An inquest later speculated that an over-the-counter motion-sickness medication had interacted badly with the custom gas mix that Richard was breathing, causing him to lose consciousness. He simply fell asleep and never woke up.

To a diving community that had honored Richard as one of its leaders, the news was shattering. Many people had come to think of him as invincible, and now he was gone. I called his family and made arrangements to personally write the obituary that would appear in *Underwater Journal*, the official PADI instructors' publication. And then I called the dive shop, wondering what else I could do.

I was thinking about the press releases and other things they might need. But they didn't mention any of that.

"I'm glad you called," the shop manager told me. "With Richard gone, we're going to be scrambling to try to cover all the classes we have scheduled. Could you take some?"

Me?

Teach?

"But I—" I began. Then I caught myself.

"Sure," I told him. "I'd be honored to."

Since that time, more students than I can remember have gone through my dive classes. I have gone on to earn PADI's Master Scuba Diver Trainer rating, and I am a specialty instructor in a number of areas. As I was sitting down to write this, someone called me to see if I would care to take a class as a Staff Instructor, the last step before being certified as a Course Director—the same thing as Richard had been, an instructor who teaches instructors. I'm thinking of doing it.

Gifts are given for a purpose, you know.

You're supposed to use them.

There are people—good, honest and well-meaning Christians—who truly believe that an atheist cannot be lead to redemption through Jesus Christ.

"You've got to be able to start somewhere," they'll tell you. "The person you're talking to has to believe in God, and they have to believe that the Bible is God's Word. Otherwise, you have nothing with which to work."

Well, that's balderdash.

And I'm the living proof.

For years—decades, really—I woke up every morning thinking that nothing awaited at the end of this life but the grave. I not only knew of the Bible, I had read it through several times, and each time had come away thinking that it was a work of great depth, and great beauty, but was no closer to truth than "Beowulf," "The Iliad," or "The Odyssey." For every Christian story—God becoming incarnate as Man, the virgin birth, the conflict between Supreme Good and consummate evil—I could cite a half dozen or more parallels in the myths and lore of various pagan cultures. I answered only to myself, I did what I pleased, and, like any man who lives without hope and leads a life with no real purpose, I was absolutely, profoundly and terribly unhappy.

All of that changed the moment that I first recognized the validity of the Bible, first realized that Jesus died on the cross in payment for my sins, and first truly understood that it was possible to repent—turn away from a sin-led life and toward a God-led life—and start over again, right with God.

And, fortunately, the people who witnessed to me were not stopped by my hesitance to believe in the existence of a Supreme Being or the validity of Scripture, because they knew that they were not the ones who were going to save me. Jesus was.

In Mark 13:34, Jesus compares Himself to a wealthy landowner who, upon leaving on a trip, gives "authority to his servants" and leaves them to carry on what he has started. The servants have, in and of themselves, no powers whatsoever. If one of them were to try, of his own volition, to purchase land, or sell a crop, he would very probably be laughed out of the marketplace— or even arrested for fraud. But, under the authority given by his master, the servant is able to act, because those with whom he deals understand that it is not his will he is conveying, but the will of the one who sent him.

And that was the case with the wise and patient people who witnessed to me. They did not worry about my preparation to hear the gospel, or their ability to convey God's plan of salvation, given my hesitance to believe. Rather, they were simply obedient to Paul's appeal in 1 Thessalonians 5:14: "Now we exhort you, brethren, warn them that are unruly, comfort the feebleminded, support the weak, be patient toward all men."

206

I'll leave it to you to decide where in that mix I belonged. But the point is, the Bible makes it clear that God wants everyone to hear the gospel. We are not to pick and choose those who'll hear our witness. It is, after all, Jesus Christ who provides the redemption. Those who convey the gospel message are merely His instruments.

In the weeks and months after I accepted Jesus Christ as my Savior, I wasn't really concerned about any of this. I didn't really care how it was that Christ's message had been brought across to me; I was too busy rejoicing that it simply had. After years of denying Christ—of denying God's very existence—my eyes had been opened to the truth, and the quality of my life had changed one hundred and eighty degrees. I had been hell-bound and damned, and now I was heaven-bound and a claimed child of the one true God. The magnitude of that change overwhelmed me. I was, in my mind, a completed work.

I never suspected at the time that I had only just begun another very important journey.

Mark 5:1–20 tells the story of how Jesus encountered, in a graveyard near the city of Gadara, an unfortunate man inhabited by literally a multitude of demons. The man was considered beyond help by the people of the area—in his madness, he exhibited strength so great that he could break free even if chained, and, as he mutilated himself with sharp fragments of stone, most people were afraid to go near him.

Not Jesus. He recognized the man's true plight immediately, commanded the spirits to leave him, and cast them into a herd of two thousand pigs, which immediately threw themselves into the sea and drowned themselves, rather than endure the demons' presence. And when the pigs' handlers told the townspeople what had happened, everyone came out to the scene, and was surprised to see the former madman "sitting, and clothed, and in his right mind" (Mark 5:15).

I see great parallels between the story of that man in Gadara and my own. I think many people, on hearing my opinions about God and Christianity, would have written me off as beyond hope.

But Jesus thought differently and, through His obedient servants, He reached me.

The change in the former madman was so great, and his gratitude so deep, that he begged Jesus to take him with Him . . . to allow him to stay in the safety and sanctity and comfort of His company (Mark 5:18).

Again, I can understand that. From the moment that I realized the truth of the gospel, from the instant that I first believed, the bosom of my Savior was where I wanted to spend the rest of my life. In 1 John 4:16, the Bible tells us that "God is love"—and I was content to spend the rest of my lifetime basking in the presence of that Love.

But Jesus had other plans for the man from Gadara. And Jesus had other plans for me.

Rather than allowing the man from Gadara to join His company of disciples, Jesus instructed the man (Mark 5:19) to "Go home to thy friends, and tell them how great things the Lord hath done for thee, and hath had compassion on thee."

The man obeyed, and the Bible records how he traveled throughout the Decapolis—a region in what is now the border area between Syria and Turkey—witnessing for Christ and reaching many people.

And in my own case, I soon found that I could not simply contain within myself the gift that God's Son had given to me. I had to tell others. I spoke, as Christ had instructed the man from Gadara, to friends and acquaintances—some of whom felt uncomfortable around Christians and distanced themselves from me. I even spoke to total strangers.

And I remember one time when, having dinner in a Japanese restaurant, I spoke to the waitress and, in a combination of English and better Japanese than I'd thought I could muster, I gave her a gospel tract and explained how she could have Christ as her Savior. Five minutes later, she was back, asking me for two more tracts. She had two friends, she told me, and she wanted them to have this great and wonderful gift as well.

And then, just nine months after I'd first accepted Christ as my Savior, I was in a church service when I felt the Lord was telling me that He wanted me to become more of an evangelist for Him. I remember thinking at the time that this could not be possible, that such work required education I did not possess . . . that I could not possibly be ready.

I even thought, jokingly, to myself, that the Lord must have been off in His aim, that the message I was receiving must have been meant for some Bible-college- or seminary-educated person in the seat behind me. And the church was packed that evening, with people sitting even in sections that normally went unused. But when I turned and peeked at the seat behind me, it was empty.

When my friend Richard took me through that course in becoming a scuba instructor, I was being trained with a purpose. An instructor teaches others how to have the same gift he or she enjoys. And, regardless of what my intentions might have been when I took the training, when Richard died, I knew that it would be selfish and wrong for me to keep what I had learned to myself. I shared it, and in sharing it, I fulfilled the purpose for which I had been trained.

"Ye are the light of the world," the Bible tells us in Matthew 5:14–15. "A city that is set on an hill cannot be hid. Neither do men light a candle, and put it under a bushel, but on a candlestick; and it giveth light unto all that are in the house."

When He was born in Bethlehem so many centuries ago, Jesus Christ came with a purpose. He came to break the bondage of sin, to give people the opportunity to have that which they could never obtain on their own—righteousness in the eyes of God and worthiness to spend eternity with Him in heaven.

And when we become Christians, we live out the rest of our interval here on earth with a purpose—to tell others about the gift that we have received, and to show them how they can have it as well.

Such a calling touches virtually every part of our lives. It requires us to live in a manner that is a testimony and a tribute to the One who saved us—loving in dealing with our friends and families, ethical in dealing with others, and concerned for the welfare of all around us, knowing that Jesus taught (Acts 20:35), "It is more blessed to give than to receive."

It requires a commitment—but not nearly the commitment that was required when the immortal, sinless God went to a cross on Calvary to die for the sins of mankind.

To become a scuba instructor, I underwent more than eighty hours of training—and that was on top of years of experience, hundreds and hundreds of dives, and no fewer than five prerequisite certification levels. It took all of that—simply so I could teach people how to safely and effectively enjoy a recreational activity.

How much preparation is needed, then, to teach people how they can receive heaven and avoid hell?

To answer that question, let me ask you this: How much time did the man from Gadara spend with Jesus and His disciples before being sent off on his mission?

The Bible does not answer that specifically, but it certainly was no longer than a few days—and it may have been only a few hours.

And that Gadarene missionary didn't even have a pocket New Testament to carry with him.

This is not to say that Bible studies and formal education are not useful to the witnessing Christian. On the contrary—the more one learns and knows, the more effectively one can answer questions, the better one is equipped to help others to grow in Christ, and the greater is one's appreciation for the depth and beauty of God's great love for us. But the fact remains that, if you have accepted Jesus Christ as your Savior, and if you understood what was told you when you did that, then you already know what you need to know to share that gift with someone else.

After all, it's not really you who's doing the talking. It's God. As the Bible explains in Matthew 10:20, whether we are wit-

nessing or defending our faith against the attacks of others, "It is not ye that speak, but the Spirit of your Father which speaketh in you."

When I took my training and testing as a scuba instructor, I had no intention of using it. I was not unique in that regard; a surprising number of people attain the instructor's rating simply to have it and never go on to teach.

As Christians, do we fare any better?

Perhaps you've heard the story about the man who applies for a job and, for a wage, simply asks the employer to pay him a penny for the first day's work and then to double his wages every day after that. The employer agrees and when, after a week on the job, the employee has received only $1.28, the employer feels certain that he has struck the bargain of a lifetime. But, after a month passes, the employer is startled to learn that, based on simple mathematical compounding, he now owes the man no less than $10,787,418.24!

On the same principle, if every Christian went out and showed just two people how they could receive Christ as their Savior, and if those two people went out and told two more, and so forth . . . then, obviously, it wouldn't be very long before there were no lost people left on earth.

But, just as obviously, that is not the case.

What difference can one person make? Well, somewhere, as I write these words, someone that I trained to dive is probably underwater right now, enjoying the ocean realm, observing the undersea environment, and acting as a steward of one of the natural gifts that God has given us.

And the once demon-possessed man from Gadara? Well, again, the Bible says that he talked about what Jesus had done for him all through the "Decapolis" (Mark 5:20), and "Decapolis" is not the name of a town but the name of a region containing ten cities—decapolis in Greek literally means "the ten cities."

One of the cities to which the Gadarene man traveled in his ministry was certainly Damascus. Damascus was the largest of the towns in the ten-city region, and to travel the Decapolis without visiting Damascus would be like traveling the cities of Illinois and not visiting Chicago—the omission would be so noteworthy that any writer would feel obliged to mention it.

So the Gadarene went to Damascus, and Christianity obviously took hold there, because so many Christians sprang up that they attracted the attention of a man named Saul, a Roman citizen who made it his business to persecute the followers of Jesus Christ. And, as Saul was traveling on the road to Damascus, he was struck blind by a visitation from Jesus Himself (Acts 9:3–9).

And then a Christian in Damascus named Ananias—very possibly a Christian who had been witnessed to by the man from Gadara himself—was told by God (Acts 9:11–16) to go and minister to Saul. And that man Saul became the apostle Paul, the author of the majority of the New Testament, and the world's first great missionary for Jesus Christ.

All, quite possibly, because one man went and told (Mark 5:19) what "great things the Lord hath done."

As for me, this book is being written because a Christian—more than one, really—had the strength and faith to witness to a skeptic. And somewhere, someone may be reading these words right now, and that person may be coming to an understanding that Christ died in payment for his sins and that eternal salvation is his, if only he will receive it.

And maybe—just maybe—that person is you.

If it is, I rejoice at your decision.

But whether you made that decision just now or long before you opened these pages, I urge you: Do not hide your light. Use your gift. It was given to you for a purpose.

Go.

Tell.

ACKNOWLEDGMENTS

Literally hundreds of people from all over the world—many of whom have never so much as met me—prayed for me and for this book as it was in progress, and for that, I am eternally grateful. The most powerful element man has ever harnessed is not nuclear energy, or invading armies, but the potent and irresistible force of Christians united in prayer.

Very early on, I shared my calling to write this book with Dr. Daniel L. Woodward, pastor of First Baptist Church in Dwight, Illinois. Dr. Woodward, the proverbial friend who sticks closer than a brother, immediately announced the news to his entire congregation, effectively burning any bridge by which I might hope to retreat. He, his wife, Cindy, and their family carefully read this work as it was in progress, and I appreciate their comments and constant encouragement.

Gloria Jasperse, of Baker Book House, became an early champion of this cause and worked many, many months—weekends and evenings included—to see it to fruition. Her patience, skill, tact, professionalism and friendship are all reflected in these pages.

Several chapters of *Wild by Nature* were written at Camp Achor, in Ypsilanti, Michigan: America's largest camp meeting east of the Mississippi. The people there fed body and soul during several happy days, and Pastor Jimmy Walker was kind enough to give up his very comfortable study for an entire week in order to provide me with a place in which to work.

Dr. Ron Martoia and Pastor Scott Hofert, of Westwinds Community Church (Jackson, Michigan); Pastor Darren Melugin of Cascades Baptist Church (also in Jackson); and Dr. John Vaprezsan and Pastor John Vaprezsan (father and son, of Metro Baptist Church in Belleville, Michigan) all read various sections of this book and brought their wealth of theological knowledge to bear upon it. Any strange fire remaining in these pages is the result, not of their review, but of the intractability of the writer. I thank all these busy men of God for adding yet another item to their burgeoning schedules without a syllable of hesitance or complaint.

As much of this writing was done from admittedly fickle memory, I checked it whenever practical against that of others who had been there for the events described. They included Scott Campbell, manager of Divers Incorporated; Dustin Clesi, owner of Steamboat Inn dive resort; Professor Bruce Groves of the University of Toledo; Cal Lee of the University of Michigan; Dr. Ed Rhudy, of Davis-Elkins College; Chuck Winger, owner of Winger & Associates, and others. I thank them for graciously lending their hands in a job that was clearly not their own.

Michelle Smart sacrificed several evenings of her time to read every word of the manuscript—including the occasional word spelled correctly—and patiently point out those parts that would start Mssrs. Webster, Strunk and White spinning in their graves. And Al Lee and Chuck Snearly, both great friends and wonderful writers, offered support and encouragement in a project which, like all books, often involved long periods of waiting and reflection.

In short, while a single name may appear on its cover, this book was very much a community effort, and I thank God for placing me in the company of such supportive and selfless people. Any good that comes from this work is purely the result of His efforts, and of theirs. Its shortcomings I claim entirely as my own.

Tom Morrisey is an active member of the Society of American Travel Writers, a teaching member of the Professional Association of Diving Instructors, and a ni-dan (second degree black belt) in Ryokukai Karate-Do, as well as an angler, shooting-sports enthusiast, motorsports enthusiast, cyclist, climber, Nordic and alpine skier, student pilot, backpacker, and cave diver. A novelist whose shorter work appears regularly in national magazines, he is also a popular Christian speaker and a lay evangelist active with youth and prison ministries.

Morrisey lives and writes on a small farm in Jackson County, Michigan.